Arcade Chaos: 30 Games That Defined an Era

Arcade chaos

Matthew taylor

Published by Matthew taylor, 2026.

ARCADE CHAOS

First edition. March 15, 2026.

ISBN: 979-8215622070

Written by Matthew taylor.

by Matthew Taylor

Introduction – Insert Coin: A Decade That Changed Everything

The 1980s did not simply produce video games. They forged a new language of imagination. They transformed spare change into adventure, flickering pixels into mythology, and bedrooms into gateways to other worlds. It was a decade of noise and neon, of joysticks gripped too tightly and CRT screens glowing in darkened rooms long after bedtime. It was a time when the impossible became playable.

At the dawn of the decade, arcades were temples of light and sound. Rows of cabinets stood like technological monoliths, their artwork bold and dramatic, their attract screens flickering with promise. Teenagers crowded around machines, studying patterns, memorising enemy behaviour, chasing high scores etched into digital stone. A single coin could buy three minutes of glory or humiliation. Every second mattered. Every mistake was visible to the watching crowd. Victory was not just about finishing a game — it was about surviving long enough to leave your initials for others to see.

The arcade boom carried forward the shockwave of late-1970s success stories, but the early 1980s intensified everything. Pac-Man became more than a game; it became a cultural phenomenon. Plush toys, cereal boxes, cartoons — a maze chase had escaped the cabinet and entered everyday life. Meanwhile, Space Invaders continued to influence design philosophy with its escalating tension and minimalist brilliance. These early giants proved that simplicity, when executed perfectly, could become timeless.

But the 1980s were not just about arcades. They were about transition.

The home console market surged, then collapsed. The infamous North American video game crash of 1983 sent shockwaves through the industry. Oversaturation, poor-quality releases, and consumer distrust nearly destroyed home gaming. Companies folded. Retailers pulled stock from shelves. For a moment, it seemed the experiment had failed.

Yet from that collapse came reinvention.

In 1985, Super Mario Bros. did not merely launch a plumber into pixelated skies — it resurrected an industry. With precise controls, imaginative level design, and hidden secrets tucked behind warp pipes and invisible blocks, it restored faith in home gaming. More importantly, it redefined what a video game could feel like. It was no longer just about reflexes. It was about discovery.

At the same time, the United Kingdom and parts of Europe were living a parallel revolution. The ZX Spectrum, Commodore 64, and Amstrad CPC transformed bedrooms into development labs. Young coders, often still in their teens, created games from scratch — designing graphics, writing music, programming logic. Gaming was not yet a corporate behemoth; it was a frontier. Creativity thrived in limitation. With kilobytes of memory and tape-loading screens that lasted minutes, developers squeezed imagination into impossibly tight spaces. Entire universes were built from colour clash and beeping sound chips.

The decade also saw the birth of genre identity. Before the 1980s, many games were variations on simple themes: shoot, dodge, score. But as technology improved, boundaries expanded. The Legend of Zelda introduced open exploration and the radical concept of saving progress. Metroid created isolation and atmosphere through environmental storytelling. Final Fantasy demonstrated that sprawling narrative adventures could exist on a cartridge. These were no longer mere diversions; they were worlds.

The 1980s also introduced personality into gaming. Characters were no longer anonymous ships or paddles. They had names, faces, quirks. Mario jumped. Link explored. Samus hunted. The player was no longer just a high score — they were an adventurer, a hero, a participant in unfolding drama. Emotional investment entered the medium.

Technological innovation accelerated at a breathtaking pace. Sprites became smoother. Scrolling became fluid. Music evolved from simple beeps to layered compositions that remain recognisable decades later. Games like Tetris proved that elegance and psychological precision could create obsession without narrative or spectacle. Meanwhile, arcade showcases such as Out Run delivered speed, colour, and fantasy in a way that felt almost cinematic.

And yet, beneath the innovation, the core magic remained simple: interactivity.

For the first time in mainstream entertainment, the audience was not passive. Players shaped outcomes. They failed and tried again. They learned patterns. They improved. Mastery was earned, not watched. Video games demanded participation. They rewarded perseverance. They punished carelessness. They invited obsession.

The 1980s also defined difficulty in a way that modern gaming rarely dares. Many titles were unforgiving, shaped by arcade economics that thrived on challenge. Three lives. No mercy. Start again. This brutality created resilience in a generation of players. Victory felt monumental because defeat was constant.

Culturally, the decade embedded gaming into identity. Arcades became social spaces. Friendships were formed over shared strategies. Rivalries burned across leaderboards. Consoles became Christmas miracles and birthday treasures. Magazine culture flourished — tips, cheat codes, pixelated screenshots analysed in forensic detail. Gaming was not just played; it was studied.

By the end of the decade, the foundation had been laid. The industry had survived collapse. It had produced mascots, genres, franchises, and technological leaps that would echo into the 1990s and beyond. What began as novelty had matured into an art form, a business empire, and a global culture.

This book explores twenty defining titles of that extraordinary decade. Each chapter will dive deeply into one game — not just its mechanics, but its context. Who created it? What limitations shaped it? Why did it resonate? How did it influence everything that followed? From maze chases to sprawling adventures, from arcade cabinets to home consoles, each game represents a milestone in the construction of modern gaming.

The 1980s were not primitive. They were foundational. Every open-world epic, every online multiplayer battle, every cinematic masterpiece released today carries DNA from those early experiments in code and colour.

Before teraflops and photorealism, there were pixels and imagination.

Before online servers, there were high-score tables.

Before vast open worlds, there were side-scrolling dreams.

And it all began with a coin, a joystick, and a screen that promised something entirely new.

Press Start.

Chapter One – Pac-Man and the Maze That Conquered the World

In 1980, arcades were dominated by war. Alien fleets descended in rigid formation. Laser fire streaked across black screens. Players defended Earth again and again from pixelated invaders. The formula was clear: shoot first, survive as long as possible, and chase the high score. Then something unexpected arrived. It did not fire bullets. It did not pilot a spaceship. It simply ate.

Pac-Man was conceived by Toru Iwatani at Namco with a simple but radical idea — create a game that would appeal to a wider audience, particularly women, who were largely ignored by the arcade industry at the time. The inspiration, according to legend, came from a pizza with a slice missing. Whether myth or marketing polish, the result was unmistakable: a yellow circle with a mouth, endlessly consuming dots in a glowing maze.

The design philosophy behind Pac-Man was revolutionary in its restraint. Instead of waves of enemies descending from above, the danger came from four distinct ghosts — Blinky, Pinky, Inky, and Clyde — each programmed with subtle behavioural differences. This was not random chaos. It was a dance of algorithms. Blinky chased relentlessly. Pinky attempted ambush. Inky behaved unpredictably. Clyde alternated between pursuit and retreat. Players who paid attention began to recognise patterns. Mastery was not about reflex alone; it was about understanding.

The maze itself became iconic. Its symmetry created clarity. Its corridors forced decision-making. Its power pellets transformed prey into predator, flipping the emotional state of the player in an instant. The sound design — the repetitive waka-waka of dot consumption — embedded itself into popular consciousness. It was simple, almost hypnotic, and perfectly tuned to the arcade environment.

But Pac-Man's success was not merely mechanical. It was cultural.

By 1981, what journalists dubbed "Pac-Man Fever" had swept across the United States and beyond. Merchandise flooded the market:

lunchboxes, bed sheets, board games, breakfast cereal, even a hit novelty song. A Saturday morning cartoon adaptation followed. The character transcended gaming and entered mainstream recognition in a way no previous arcade creation had achieved. For the first time, a video game mascot was a household name.

Technologically, Pac-Man demonstrated how personality could emerge from limitation. The hardware was modest, yet the ghost AI felt alive. The difficulty curve was carefully constructed, gradually increasing speed and aggression. And then there was the kill screen — the infamous level 256 glitch, where corrupted memory caused half the screen to become an unplayable jumble of symbols. It was not designed as an ending, but it became a legendary milestone for elite players chasing perfection.

In the broader historical context, Pac-Man marked a turning point. It proved that games did not need violence to be compelling. It showed that character design mattered. It demonstrated the power of branding before the industry fully understood what branding meant. And it expanded the demographic reach of arcades, inviting new audiences into what had been a largely male-dominated space.

The economic impact was staggering. Pac-Man became one of the highest-grossing arcade games of all time, generating billions in quarters during its peak years. Arcades reorganised their floors to accommodate demand. Cabinets were converted into Pac-Man units. Clones and imitators followed, attempting to replicate the maze formula with varying degrees of success.

Yet beyond sales figures and merchandise, Pac-Man's true legacy lies in its psychology. The game creates tension without aggression. It traps the player in confined spaces with intelligent pursuers. It rewards pattern recognition and punishes hesitation. Even today, decades later, the sensation of being cornered by converging ghosts still produces a spike of adrenaline.

Pac-Man also represents something more intangible — innocence. Its bright colours and abstract design feel playful rather than threatening. It belongs to a time when the boundaries of gaming were still undefined, when experimentation could yield global phenomena. The character's simplicity allowed imagination to fill in the blanks. Was Pac-Man smiling? Panicking? Determined? The player projected emotion onto a moving mouth.

As the 1980s unfolded, games would grow more complex, more narrative-driven, more technologically ambitious. But Pac-Man remains a symbol of purity in design. No tutorials. No sprawling maps. No save files. Just a maze, four ghosts, and a challenge that escalates until human capability reaches its limit.

In many ways, Pac-Man established the blueprint for longevity in gaming: easy to learn, brutally difficult to master. It invited beginners while rewarding obsession. It created community through competition. It became a shared cultural touchstone.

The maze was small. The impact was enormous.

The 1980s had found their icon.

Chapter Two - Space Invaders and the War That Built the Arcade

Before mascots. Before narratives. Before scrolling landscapes and hidden warp zones, there was a black screen and an approaching formation.

Space Invaders did not technically begin in the 1980s — it was released in 1978 — but its dominance bled heavily into the early years of the decade, shaping arcade economics, hardware design, and player psychology in ways that would define everything that followed. If Pac-Man humanised gaming, Space Invaders industrialised it.

Created by Tomohiro Nishikado for Taito, Space Invaders was born from limitation. Nishikado had initially attempted to design a more complex shooting game but was restricted by hardware incapable of rendering fast-moving objects with multiple detailed sprites. The solution was ingenious: slow everything down. Instead of enemies diving and weaving, they would march downward in rigid formation. The result was not dullness — it was dread.

The aliens moved as a collective. A synchronised descent. A tightening noose.

What players discovered almost immediately was that the game became faster as the invaders were destroyed. Fewer enemies meant less processing strain on the hardware, which inadvertently increased speed. This was not originally intended as a dynamic difficulty system, yet it became one of the most brilliant accidental mechanics in gaming history. The tension escalated as success increased. The better you performed, the more frantic the game became.

That rising tempo — punctuated by the now legendary four-note bass pulse — created one of the first examples of interactive music design. The sound wasn't background decoration. It reflected the threat level. As the invaders sped up, so did the heartbeat of the machine.

Arcade operators quickly realised they were witnessing something unprecedented. In Japan, Space Invaders cabinets were reportedly in such demand that arcades were dedicated entirely to the game. Though stories of nationwide coin shortages are likely exaggerated, there is no doubt the game generated extraordinary revenue. In the United States and Europe, it ignited what became known as the “golden age of arcades.”

The gameplay was deceptively simple. A lone cannon at the bottom of the screen. Barriers for temporary protection. Rows of descending aliens. Occasional mystery ships gliding across the top for bonus points. But within that simplicity lay deep strategy. Skilled players learned to manipulate the formation, carving controlled tunnels through the invaders to manage descent speed. Others discovered the “last invader” phenomenon — when a single alien remained, it would move at terrifying speed, transforming the screen into a high-stakes duel.

Space Invaders was also one of the first games to foster widespread competitive culture. High-score chasing became a communal obsession. Initials carved into leaderboards became marks of local fame. Players studied patterns, timing, and shot rhythm with forensic intensity.

When the game arrived on home systems, its impact multiplied.

The 1980 port for the Atari 2600 became the console's first true "killer app." Console sales reportedly quadrupled following its release. For many households, Space Invaders justified the purchase of a home gaming system. Though technically inferior to the arcade version, the port captured enough of the experience to bring the alien invasion into living rooms across the world.

Different variations emerged across platforms — the Atari 5200, the Nintendo Entertainment System (Famicom in Japan), and numerous home computers including the Commodore 64 and ZX Spectrum. Each version carried slight differences in speed, colour palette, and sound, but the core tension remained intact.

Clones flooded the market. Galaxian, Phoenix, and countless lesser-known titles borrowed the descending enemy template. The fixed shooter genre was born almost overnight.

There were also myths, secrets, and competitive exploits.

In the arcade version, advanced players discovered safe spots — positions where alien shots would rarely strike due to programmed firing patterns. These were not invincible zones but offered slight statistical advantage. On certain home ports, players uncovered predictable enemy firing logic that could be manipulated. Score-maxing became an art form, with marathon sessions lasting hours as players sought theoretical maximums.

The psychology of Space Invaders deserves particular examination. Unlike later shooters that empowered players with mobility and spectacle, this game constrained movement to a horizontal plane. There was no escape upward, no retreat. The enemy did not need to destroy you outright; it only needed to reach the bottom of the screen. The pressure was constant, existential. The game introduced the concept of inevitable encroachment — survival against a force that would not stop.

Culturally, Space Invaders also sparked early moral panic. Media outlets questioned whether arcades were addictive environments corrupting youth. Stories circulated of students skipping school to play. Newspapers debated whether video games were a harmless pastime or a social threat. This pattern — technological innovation followed by cultural anxiety — would repeat throughout gaming history.

From a design perspective, Space Invaders established foundational principles:

Clear objective.

Escalating difficulty.

Score as status.

Immediate restart upon failure.

It created the arcade loop that defined early 1980s design philosophy — short, intense sessions engineered for repeat play and coin consumption.

Technologically, it also pushed hardware forward. Nishikado had to design custom hardware to realise his vision, effectively creating a platform around the game itself. This blending of software and hardware innovation became a hallmark of arcade development throughout the decade.

As the 1980s progressed, games would grow more colourful, more complex, more character-driven. Yet Space Invaders remained the blueprint for tension and pacing. Its DNA can be traced through shoot 'em ups, tower defence games, and even survival horror — the concept of an advancing threat growing more dangerous as it diminishes is timeless.

The imagery remains iconic: pixelated aliens descending in mechanical unison. A lone cannon firing upward. Barriers crumbling under relentless assault.

It was minimal. It was repetitive. It was hypnotic.

And it built an industry.

Space Invaders did not just entertain. It proved that video games could dominate public spaces, generate enormous profit, shape youth culture, and create a competitive ecosystem around digital skill. It turned arcades into battlegrounds and players into defenders of Earth.

The war may have been pixelated.

But its impact was very real.

Chapter Three - Donkey Kong and the Birth of a Hero

By 1981, the arcade industry was hungry for the next phenomenon. Space shooters ruled the floor. Fixed screens, high scores, alien invasions — the formula worked, but it was becoming predictable. Into this landscape stepped a wooden construction site, a furious ape, and a carpenter who would eventually become the most recognisable character in gaming history.

Donkey Kong was not simply another arcade release. It was a turning point. It introduced narrative framing, character personality, and vertical platforming in a way no previous game had achieved. It also saved Nintendo's American division from potential collapse.

At the time, Nintendo was not yet a global video game powerhouse. The company had roots in playing cards and toys. Its early arcade efforts had failed to capture sustained attention in the United States. Thousands of unsold cabinets sat in warehouses. The pressure was immense. Nintendo needed something different — something memorable.

The task fell to a young designer named Shigeru Miyamoto, who had little programming experience but a deep understanding of visual storytelling. Inspired partly by Western cartoons and even the dynamic between Popeye, Bluto, and Olive Oyl (a license Nintendo had failed to secure), Miyamoto reworked the concept into something original: a giant ape kidnaps a woman, and a determined everyman climbs a structure to rescue her.

That everyman was originally called Jumpman.

The genius of Donkey Kong lies in its layered simplicity. The goal is straightforward: ascend platforms, avoid obstacles, rescue the captive Pauline. But the structure of the game was revolutionary. Instead of one endlessly repeating screen, Donkey Kong featured multiple distinct stages — the barrel stage, the conveyor belt stage, the elevator stage, and the rivet stage. Each required new tactics and pattern recognition.

This was one of the earliest examples of level progression in arcade design. The game told a story through movement. The ape climbed higher. The structure changed. The player followed.

Mechanically, Donkey Kong refined the concept of jumping as a primary verb. Earlier games had included jumping, but here it became precise and central. Timing mattered. Distance mattered. A mistimed leap meant plummeting to death. The arc of Jumpman's jump was carefully tuned — stiff compared to later Mario titles, but groundbreaking at the time.

The hardware limitations also shaped design brilliance. The angled girders of the first stage were not purely aesthetic; they allowed barrels to roll in unpredictable patterns, increasing tension. Fireballs emerged from oil drums. Conveyors reversed direction. Every hazard felt alive within the rigid constraints of early 80s circuitry.

Then there was Donkey Kong himself.

Unlike the faceless invaders of previous hits, this antagonist had personality. He pounded his chest. He grinned. He moved with purpose. The rivalry felt personal. Players were not defending Earth — they were climbing toward confrontation.

The difficulty was unforgiving. Limited lives. No continues in the early arcade model. Escalating speed. The infamous kill screen at level 22 — caused by a timer overflow bug — rendered the game unwinnable beyond a certain point. Like Pac-Man's level 256, this glitch became legend among elite competitors chasing perfect scores.

Donkey Kong also cemented the high-score culture that defined the golden age of arcades. Decades later, competitive score-chasing would become the subject of documentaries and rivalries, proving the game's enduring influence on gaming subculture.

When Donkey Kong was ported to home systems, it became a system seller. The ColecoVision version was remarkably faithful to the arcade original and was bundled with the console, boosting hardware sales dramatically. Ports also appeared on the Atari 2600 and numerous home computers, though many suffered from graphical and mechanical compromises.

One curious footnote in console history came with the Nintendo Entertainment System (Famicom in Japan). Donkey Kong was among its early titles, helping establish Nintendo's identity before the arrival of Super Mario Bros.

Cheat culture around Donkey Kong was less about secret codes and more about pattern exploitation. Skilled players developed precise routes — manipulating barrel behaviour by climbing ladders at exact moments, positioning Jumpman to influence enemy spawn logic. Advanced tactics included "hammer efficiency" — using the temporary invincibility power-up strategically to maximise points without wasting time.

Beyond mechanics and competition, Donkey Kong's true legacy lies in character evolution.

Jumpman was later renamed Mario, reportedly after Mario Segale, the landlord of Nintendo of America's warehouse. That moustached carpenter would soon trade construction sites for mushroom kingdoms. Donkey Kong himself would transform from villain to antihero in later years. Entire franchises were born from this single cabinet.

The game also marked the beginning of Nintendo's design philosophy — tight controls, memorable characters, escalating challenge, and intuitive mechanics layered over hidden depth. That philosophy would carry through decades of innovation.

Culturally, Donkey Kong helped shift the perception of video games from abstract score machines to narrative experiences. The opening animation — brief as it was — established context. A conflict. A goal. A relationship between characters. It may seem primitive now, but in 1981 it was groundbreaking.

And perhaps most importantly, Donkey Kong proved that video games could create icons.

Not spaceships.

Not paddles.

Characters.

The 1980s would go on to produce many legends, but here — on a stack of pixelated girders beneath a grinning ape — a hero was born.

And he was just getting started.

Chapter Four - Frogger and the Art of Crossing Chaos

If Space Invaders was about defence and Donkey Kong was about ascent, then Frogger was about survival through timing. No weapons. No ladders. No fireballs. Just a small green frog attempting to cross a deadly road and a treacherous river.

Released in 1981 by Konami and distributed in North America by Sega, Frogger distilled tension into movement. The premise was deceptively simple: guide five frogs safely home by navigating traffic and leaping across floating logs, turtles, and crocodiles. Yet within that simplicity lay a masterclass in rhythm, spatial awareness, and escalating pressure.

The lower half of the screen was mechanical terror — cars, trucks, and racing vehicles moved horizontally at varying speeds. The upper half replaced steel with water, but danger remained constant. Miss a log and you drowned. Land on a turtle that submerges and you disappeared beneath the surface. Linger too long and the timer punished hesitation. Every second counted.

Frogger's brilliance lies in lane psychology. Each row behaved differently. Some lanes moved quickly but with wide gaps. Others crawled slowly but were densely packed. Players had to read patterns in real time, calculating movement several seconds ahead. It was less about reflex and more about anticipation.

Unlike earlier fixed shooters, Frogger forced vertical progress. You were always moving forward — or attempting to. The goal was not infinite survival but successful completion of structured objectives. Once five frogs were home, the level increased in difficulty. Traffic sped up. Gaps narrowed. Hazards multiplied. The river introduced new enemies — snakes resting on logs, alligators lurking at endpoints.

From a design perspective, Frogger demonstrated how environmental hazards could replace traditional enemies. The cars were not thinking adversaries, yet they created relentless tension. The river platforms were not hostile by intention, yet they demanded precision. The world itself was the antagonist.

The arcade cabinet art reflected this colourful danger — bright greens and yellows, cartoonish vehicles, exaggerated hazards. The sound design was sparse but effective. Each movement felt deliberate. Each collision was final.

Frogger became one of the most ported games of the early 1980s. It appeared on the Atari 2600, where hardware limitations simplified graphics but preserved core mechanics. It thrived on the ColecoVision and the Commodore 64, each offering varying degrees of fidelity to the arcade original. In the UK, home computer versions on the ZX Spectrum and Amstrad CPC became household staples.

Interestingly, Frogger's gameplay translated exceptionally well to home systems because it relied more on timing than graphical spectacle. Even with reduced sprite detail, the tension remained intact.

There were no official cheat codes in the arcade version — the era predated widespread code-based manipulation — but players developed strategies that bordered on exploitation. Experienced competitors would "lane memorise," recognising safe entry points that reliably aligned with vehicle patterns. Others discovered optimal pause moments at screen edges to reset mental timing before making the next dash.

One subtle design element often overlooked is Frogger's use of endpoints. The five home slots at the top were not identical. Landing on certain slots yielded bonus points. Capturing flies for extra score required risky positioning. Avoiding crocodile heads masquerading as safe logs required split-second recognition. The game rewarded players who balanced speed with greed.

Culturally, Frogger became iconic partly because of its universal theme. Everyone understands crossing traffic. Everyone understands the danger of misjudging speed. The abstraction made it relatable. It also found a strange immortality in pop culture references, appearing in television, comedy routines, and nostalgic retrospectives decades later.

From a broader historical perspective, Frogger demonstrated that games did not need narrative complexity or character depth to endure. Its protagonist had no backstory. No emotional arc. Yet the struggle felt personal. Each failed attempt created a micro-drama of near success or sudden catastrophe.

Technically, the game also refined collision detection. The precise alignment required to land on moving objects demanded reliable hitboxes — something early games often handled inconsistently. Frogger's fairness made its difficulty addictive rather than frustrating.

The increasing speed across levels mirrored the escalating tempo of early arcade design philosophy. Like Space Invaders, success bred chaos. But unlike shooters, Frogger's chaos was layered. The player was not eliminating threats — merely navigating through them. That shift in agency was important. It introduced the concept of traversal as gameplay focus.

Frogger also hinted at something that would become more pronounced later in the decade: games about movement rather than destruction. Platformers, exploration titles, and adventure games would all build upon the idea that the act of navigating space could be compelling enough on its own.

There is something almost philosophical about Frogger. The frog is small. The world is indifferent. Traffic does not slow. The river does not wait. You move or you perish. It is timing against inevitability.

By today's standards, it may seem quaint. But in 1981, guiding that fragile frog across chaos felt monumental. The cabinet drew crowds. The tension was visible on players' faces. A single mistake — a single misjudged leap — ended everything.

No aliens.

No apes.

No heroes.

Just a frog, a road, a river — and a lesson in precision that defined an era.

And the crossings were only getting harder.

Chapter Five - Galaga and the Perfection of the Shooter

By 1981, the fixed shooter was already a proven formula. Space Invaders had laid the groundwork. Clones and competitors flooded arcades. But then Namco released something that didn't just copy the template — it refined it into near perfection.

Galaga was not revolutionary in concept. A lone starfighter at the bottom of the screen. Waves of descending alien enemies. Projectiles filling the darkness. Yet everything about Galaga felt smoother, faster, more dynamic. Where Space Invaders marched, Galaga swarmed.

The first thing players noticed was movement. Enemies didn't simply descend in rigid rows. They swooped in elaborate patterns, spiralling and diving before locking into formation. The screen felt alive. Instead of a single advancing wall, players faced individual threats breaking formation to attack aggressively.

This subtle shift transformed the psychology of the shooter.

In Space Invaders, tension came from inevitability. In Galaga, tension came from unpredictability.

The enemy behaviour was programmed with deliberate choreography. Waves entered in patterns that rewarded memorisation but punished complacency. The “bee,” “butterfly,” and “boss Galaga” enemy types each had distinct attack styles and scoring values. Destroying enemies in specific formations granted bonus points, encouraging precision over reckless firing.

Then came Galaga’s masterstroke: the capture mechanic.

Certain boss enemies would fire a tractor beam. If the player’s ship was caught, it would be captured and absorbed into the enemy formation. This created a devastating setback — reduced firepower and increased vulnerability. But the system offered redemption. If the player managed to shoot down the boss while avoiding destroying their captured ship, it would be freed and dock alongside the original craft, creating a dual fighter with double firepower.

Risk and reward were intertwined.

Sacrifice a life deliberately to gain greater firepower later? Or play conservatively and avoid the gamble?

This mechanic introduced strategic depth rarely seen in early arcade shooters. It added emotion to loss. Losing a ship wasn't merely subtraction — it was motivation to reclaim power.

Galaga also refined the concept of the "challenge stage." After certain waves, enemies would fly in elaborate patterns without firing, allowing players to shoot for bonus points without threat. These intermissions were both breathers and score opportunities. They added pacing — a rhythm between chaos and precision.

Technologically, Galaga benefited from more advanced hardware than its predecessors. Sprites were more detailed. Colours were richer. Movement was smoother. The sound design —

sharp firing effects and celebratory tones for successful formations — reinforced reward loops.

In arcades, Galaga cabinets quickly became fixtures. The attract mode's bright patterns and sound effects pulled in crowds. Its difficulty curve was punishing but fair. Unlike some contemporaries, it rarely felt cheap. Death usually resulted from misjudgment, not random chaos.

As with other arcade giants, Galaga was ported widely. Versions appeared on the Atari 7800, Nintendo Entertainment System, and numerous home computers including the Commodore 64 and MSX systems. While some home ports struggled to replicate the fluidity of the arcade original, the core mechanics translated remarkably well.

The NES version in particular became a staple of 1980s living rooms. Though slightly simplified, it maintained the capture mechanic and challenge stages, preserving what made Galaga distinctive.

Cheat culture around Galaga developed differently than in other games. The arcade version had no built-in cheat codes, but advanced players exploited enemy dive patterns to manipulate screen flow. One notorious technique involved leaving a single harmless enemy alive on certain stages to extend playtime and maximise score potential.

Later home console versions introduced hidden features. On some ports, holding specific button combinations during startup altered enemy patterns or provided small advantages — though these were more Easter eggs than full cheats.

Galaga's competitive scene endured long after the golden age of arcades faded. High-score competitions became legendary. Marathon sessions lasting hours pushed human endurance. Because the game loop eventually repeats with increasing speed, elite players developed intense memorisation strategies to survive into extraordinarily high levels.

From a design standpoint, Galaga perfected several principles:

- Individualised enemy behaviour

- Mid-game strategic risk mechanics
- Reward-focused challenge stages
- Clear visual and audio feedback

It represented evolutionary refinement rather than radical innovation. And sometimes refinement is what defines greatness.

Culturally, Galaga symbolised the maturation of arcade design. The early experimental chaos of late-70s gaming was giving way to carefully tuned systems. Developers understood player psychology more deeply. They understood pacing. They understood reward cycles.

And importantly, Galaga felt fair.

The 1980s were filled with brutally difficult games, some bordering on punishing. Galaga's challenge was intense but readable. When you died, you understood why. That clarity built loyalty.

Even decades later, Galaga machines remain fixtures in retro arcades. The core loop is timeless. Move. Fire. Dodge. Reclaim your captured ship. Chase the high score.

It did not need narrative.

It did not need a mascot.

It only needed perfect execution.

And in 1981, Galaga delivered it.

The fixed shooter had reached its peak.

But at home, something new was beginning to stir — a jungle, a whip, and the promise of adventure beyond the arcade walls.

Chapter Six – Pitfall! and the Birth of the Console Adventure

By 1982, arcades still dominated the public imagination, but something quieter — and arguably more important — was happening in living rooms. The home console was no longer a novelty. It was becoming a battleground. And into that battleground swung a vine, carrying one of the most influential games ever made for a cartridge-based system.

Pitfall! was not simply a success for the Atari 2600. It was proof that a home console could deliver a genuine sense of adventure.

Created by David Crane at Activision, Pitfall! pushed the Atari 2600 far beyond what most believed it could achieve. The hardware was notoriously limited — minimal memory, primitive sprite capabilities, severe graphical constraints. Yet Crane managed to create a sprawling jungle world containing 255 interconnected screens. On a system many assumed could barely handle a single repeating playfield.

The technical achievement alone deserves attention.

Crane developed a display kernel so efficient that it allowed for smooth horizontal scrolling between screens — something rarely seen on the Atari 2600. Rather than rely on brute-force memory usage, he engineered a procedural system to generate environments dynamically. The jungle was not stored in full; it was assembled in real time using clever programming shortcuts.

But technology alone does not create legend. Pitfall!'s true power lay in its design.

You played as Pitfall Harry — a pixelated explorer navigating a treacherous jungle filled with hazards. Swinging on vines over crocodile-infested pits. Leaping over rolling logs. Avoiding scorpions. Diving into underground tunnels. The goal was clear: collect 32 hidden treasures within a 20-minute time limit.

This was not a score-chasing arcade port. This was structured exploration.

For perhaps the first time on a home console, players felt as though they were journeying through a coherent world. The jungle screens were connected logically. Underground tunnels provided shortcuts, allowing strategic navigation. Risk could be balanced against time. Every decision mattered.

The time limit introduced tension without forcing constant enemy aggression. Unlike arcade shooters that demanded perpetual reflex, Pitfall! encouraged planning. Should you brave the surface hazards or descend into darker, riskier underground passages to save time?

The movement mechanics were precise for their era. Harry's jump arc was carefully tuned. Vine swinging required timing rather than button mashing. Crocodiles opened and closed their mouths in predictable rhythms — players learned to watch, wait, and leap.

There were no traditional cheat codes in the original cartridge, but players quickly discovered patterns. The jungle layout, though vast, followed a deterministic sequence. Dedicated players memorised optimal routes, maximising treasure collection while minimising risk. Speedrunning —

though not yet named as such — was quietly being born in living rooms.

The cultural timing of Pitfall! was also significant. Released just before the North American video game crash of 1983, it became one of the Atari 2600's best-selling titles, moving millions of copies. It stood as a high-water mark for what the console could achieve before market oversaturation and low-quality releases damaged consumer confidence.

Activision itself represented a shift in industry structure. Formed by former Atari employees seeking recognition and royalties for their work, it was one of the first third-party developers. Pitfall! symbolised the growing power of independent creativity within the gaming ecosystem.

Ports and sequels followed. Pitfall II: Lost Caverns expanded the formula with more complex level design and even an advanced sound chip built directly into the cartridge — an extraordinary move for the time. Versions appeared on home computers such as the Commodore 64 and the

Apple II, each adding subtle improvements in audio and colour depth.

Yet it is the original that remains iconic.

From a design perspective, Pitfall! introduced several enduring principles:

- Non-linear exploration
- Time management as pressure mechanic
- Environmental hazards over enemy combat
- Hidden collectibles as objective

It laid conceptual groundwork for future platformers and adventure games. Without Pitfall!, it is difficult to imagine the smooth side-scrolling triumph of Super Mario Bros. arriving in quite the same form.

There is also something important about Pitfall!'s tone. It was not about saving a princess or defeating aliens. It was about treasure hunting. Discovery. Exploration. It tapped into the romanticised adventure spirit of pulp fiction and Saturday matinee serials. The jungle was dangerous but inviting.

Technically, Pitfall! proved that memory limitations could inspire elegance rather than restrict ambition. The Atari 2600's constraints forced developers to think economically. Every byte mattered. Every pixel counted. This era produced a generation of programmers who treated optimisation as art.

The difficulty was measured rather than brutal. Failure often resulted from mistimed jumps rather than overwhelming enemy fire. The learning curve encouraged persistence rather than coin-fed repetition. It was a home experience — something to master over evenings and weekends.

Looking back, Pitfall! represents a quiet revolution. While arcades blazed with spectacle, this cartridge suggested that consoles could offer sustained journeys. It hinted at worlds larger than a single screen. It hinted at narrative, even if only implied.

And crucially, it demonstrated that adventure could fit inside 4 kilobytes of memory.

The jungle may have been pixelated.

But for millions of players in 1982, it felt endless.

And the home console was just getting started.

Chapter Seven - Pole Position and the Illusion of Speed

By 1982, arcades had mastered aliens, jungles, and construction sites. But one sensation remained elusive: speed. Not the abstract speed of falling blocks or diving enemies — real, white-knuckle velocity. The kind that makes your stomach tighten as the world blurs past.

Then came Pole Position.

Developed by Namco and distributed in North America by Atari, Pole Position did something radical for its time: it attempted simulation. It was not just about avoiding obstacles or racing in circles. It placed players on a real-world-inspired Formula One track — Fuji Speedway — and demanded technical precision.

The cabinet itself was part of the experience. Many arcades housed the deluxe sit-down version, complete with steering wheel, accelerator, brake pedal, and gear shifter. This was not a joystick and button affair. It was physical. Players leaned into corners. They corrected oversteer. They braked late and sometimes too hard. The machine roared back with engine sounds that felt mechanical rather than abstract.

Graphically, Pole Position was groundbreaking. Using advanced sprite-scaling techniques and a pseudo-3D perspective, the road appeared to stretch into the distance. Corners curved convincingly. Trackside billboards flashed by with branded advertisements — a novelty at the time. The illusion of depth created immersion unmatched by earlier racing attempts.

Unlike earlier top-down racers, Pole Position used a third-person chase camera view. This perspective became the standard for racing games for decades. Players saw their car from behind, watching it shrink slightly as it sped forward. It felt dynamic. It felt modern.

But the game was not simply spectacle.

It was structured around a qualifying lap followed by a championship race. The first objective was to complete the time trial within a strict limit to earn a starting position. Fail to qualify, and the game ended immediately. This added pressure before the race even began.

During the main event, players navigated tight corners, managed acceleration carefully, and avoided collisions with rival cars. Crashing was punishing — your car exploded in dramatic pixelated fire, costing precious seconds. Too many mistakes, and the countdown timer expired.

Pole Position introduced realism into arcade gaming. Cars handled differently depending on speed. Enter a corner too fast and you spun out. Brake too aggressively and you lost momentum. The game rewarded discipline over recklessness.

The difficulty curve was steep but fair. As players improved, lap times tightened. Mastery meant understanding the track intimately — knowing exactly when to ease off the accelerator before a bend and when to push for maximum straight-line speed.

From a technological standpoint, Pole Position pushed arcade hardware significantly forward. It was among the first games to use 16-bit graphics processing in arcades, enabling smoother scaling and more complex rendering. The sprite-scaling technique created the illusion of distance without true 3D modelling — a trick that would influence racing and driving games throughout the decade.

The game was ported to numerous home systems, including the Atari 2600, Atari 5200, and home computers like the Commodore 64. Predictably, many of these ports struggled to replicate the arcade's fluidity and scale. The Atari 2600 version, in particular, reduced the experience to simplified graphics and more rigid movement.

Yet despite technical compromises, the core design translated well. The time trial structure and track memorisation remained intact. Players at home could still experience a version of the arcade thrill.

There were no official cheat codes in the arcade release, but dedicated players discovered subtle exploits. Skilled drivers learned that certain off-road shortcuts could be taken at slight angles without triggering a crash, shaving valuable milliseconds. Others mastered “late braking” techniques — pushing corners to their absolute limit without spinning out. These were not programmed cheats but mechanical optimisations born from obsessive practice.

Culturally, Pole Position reflected a growing appetite for realism in gaming. It tapped into the global popularity of Formula One racing. The licensed track name and sponsor billboards gave the illusion of authenticity. It hinted at a future where video games would simulate real-world experiences rather than abstract them.

The cabinet’s presence in arcades also shifted social dynamics. Unlike single-joystick games, Pole Position physically occupied space. Players queued behind the seat, watching lap times and critiquing driving lines. It was less about high-score initials and more about performance metrics. Speed became status.

Economically, Pole Position became one of the highest-grossing arcade games of 1983. Its success inspired a wave of racing titles throughout the mid-80s, many attempting to replicate its pseudo-3D road rendering.

From a design perspective, Pole Position introduced several enduring innovations:

- Qualifying rounds before main gameplay
- Realistic physics-inspired handling
- Third-person chase camera perspective
- Branded in-game advertising

It proved that arcades could deliver experiences beyond abstract challenge — they could simulate aspiration. For many players, sitting in that cabinet was as close as they would come to driving a Formula One car.

And importantly, it showed that immersion could be engineered not just through story, but through sensation.

The engine roared.

The timer ticked down.

The corner approached faster than expected.

Brake too late — and you explode.

In 1982, that explosion felt revolutionary.

But even as racing games pushed toward realism, another arcade machine was preparing to redefine spectacle entirely — not through speed, but through animation that looked almost impossibly alive.

Chapter Eight – Dragon's Lair and the Laserdisc Gamble

By 1983, arcades were louder, brighter, and more competitive than ever. Hardware was advancing rapidly. Sprite scaling had created the illusion of speed. Platformers were introducing narrative framing. Shooters had refined tension into precision. But one machine stood apart from everything else on the arcade floor.

It didn't look like a traditional video game.

It looked like a cartoon come to life.

Dragon's Lair was less an incremental improvement and more a technological gamble. Developed by Cinematronics and animated by former Disney animator Don Bluth, Dragon's Lair used laserdisc technology to display full-motion animated scenes — something almost unheard of in arcades at the time.

The effect was staggering.

Instead of pixelated sprites moving against simple backgrounds, players saw hand-drawn animation with fluid movement and expressive characters. The hero, Dirk the Daring, blinked, stumbled, and flailed with personality. The dragon

Singe coiled and roared. The environments shimmered with gothic detail.

In 1983, this felt like science fiction.

But beneath the animated spectacle lay a very different kind of gameplay.

Dragon's Lair was not about exploration or free movement. It was about timing. The game operated through quick-time events long before that term existed. At specific moments, players had to input the correct directional movement or press the action button within a split-second window. Failure resulted in elaborate death sequences — often humorous, always dramatic.

This design divided players.

Some were mesmerised by the animation and cinematic presentation. Others were frustrated by what felt like trial-and-error gameplay. Unlike traditional arcade games that allowed continuous control, Dragon's Lair demanded memorisation. Players learned sequences through repetition, remembering when to move left, right, up, or strike.

It was, in essence, an interactive cartoon with strict choreography.

Technologically, the laserdisc system stored video footage rather than traditional sprite data. This allowed unprecedented visual fidelity but introduced fragility. The machines were notoriously temperamental. Laserdisc players could skip, misread frames, or fail entirely under heavy arcade usage. Maintenance became a serious concern for operators.

Yet the risk paid off — at least initially.

Dragon's Lair became an instant attraction. Crowds gathered not only to play but to watch. The cabinet itself, with its bright medieval artwork and large screen, commanded attention. Even those who never inserted a coin were captivated by the animated deaths and dramatic escapes.

The difficulty was brutal.

Timing windows were narrow. Feedback was minimal. Many players died within seconds of starting. This short playtime actually benefited arcade economics — more coins per minute. But it also created a perception that success was less about skill and more about memorisation.

There were no cheat codes in the arcade version, but pattern memorisation became the dominant strategy. Dedicated players mapped out correct input sequences for every room. Eventually, elite competitors could complete the entire game in a single run — an impressive feat of memory rather than reflex.

Home ports were attempted on systems such as the Nintendo Entertainment System and home computers like the Commodore 64. However, without laserdisc capability, these versions were dramatically simplified. The NES version reimagined Dragon's Lair as a more traditional side-scrolling platformer, sacrificing animation fidelity for playability.

These ports revealed something important: the magic of Dragon's Lair was inseparable from its technology. Without the full animation, the concept felt diminished.

Culturally, Dragon's Lair symbolised the peak — and fragility — of arcade ambition just before the crash of 1983. The industry was expanding rapidly, perhaps too rapidly. Laserdisc games were expensive to produce and maintain. When the market collapsed under the weight of oversaturation and declining consumer confidence, such costly experiments became difficult to sustain.

Yet Dragon's Lair left a lasting legacy.

It introduced cinematic presentation into mainstream gaming. It demonstrated that video games could aspire to animated storytelling. It blurred the line between film and interactivity — a concept that would resurface repeatedly in later decades, from CD-ROM adventures to full-motion video experiments of the 1990s.

It also highlighted a crucial tension in game design: spectacle versus agency.

Was Dragon's Lair truly a game in the traditional sense? Or was it a reactive experience dressed as one? The debate still echoes today in discussions about heavily scripted interactive media.

From a visual standpoint, however, its impact was undeniable. For many players in 1983, Dragon's Lair represented the future. If games could look like this now, what would they look like in ten years?

Ironically, while Dragon's Lair dazzled with animation, the broader industry was heading toward crisis. The North American video game crash loomed. Arcades would suffer. Home console trust would erode. Many companies would not survive.

Dragon's Lair was both a high point and a warning — ambition unrestrained by economic reality.

Still, for a moment in 1983, it felt like stepping inside a Saturday morning cartoon.

Dirk stumbled forward.

The dragon roared.

The screen flashed.

Press left — now.

Or die spectacularly.

And in that split second between animation and input, the 1980s revealed just how far imagination could stretch.

But across the world, in a Soviet research lab, a different kind of masterpiece was quietly taking shape — one that needed no animation, no spectacle, no dragon.

Only falling blocks.

Chapter Nine – Tetris and the Geometry of Obsession

While arcades dazzled with lasers, speed, and animated heroics, a quiet storm was forming in a small office in the Soviet Union. In 1984, Tetris emerged not from a corporate design studio or arcade powerhouse, but from the mind of Alexey Pajitnov, a computer scientist working at the Dorodnitsyn Computing Centre in Moscow. Its brilliance was deceptively simple: falling shapes that needed to be arranged. Nothing more. Nothing less.

The pieces — known as tetrominoes — each consisted of four connected blocks, falling one at a time from the top of the screen. The player's task was to rotate and position them to create solid horizontal lines. Complete a line, and it disappears. Fail, and the stack grows, inch by inch, until the screen overflows and the game ends.

From a technical standpoint, Tetris was elegant. Pajitnov wrote it for the Elektronika 60, a modest Soviet computer with minimal graphics and no sound. Yet even in its primitive form, the game's addictive potential was clear. The pieces fell at a measured pace, gradually accelerating. Each successful line provided instant gratification, yet the growing stack created escalating tension.

Unlike arcade shooters or platformers, Tetris was not about reflex alone. It was about planning, pattern recognition, and foresight. Players learned to manipulate "Tetris theory" — creating gaps that could only be filled by specific shapes, sacrificing immediate completion for long-term score efficiency. Each decision carried weight. One misaligned tetromino could ruin an entire strategy.

Tetris spread slowly at first, passed among colleagues on floppy disks. It wasn't initially monetized; there were no cabinets, no cartridges, no high-score initials. Yet word of mouth ensured rapid adoption. By the late 1980s, ports had appeared on the Nintendo Game Boy, IBM PCs, Commodore 64s, and countless home computers. Each platform introduced slight differences in speed, control, or scoring, but the core design remained intact.

The Game Boy port, paired with the launch of the handheld itself in 1989, is credited with globalising Tetris. Millions carried a puzzle in their pocket — a portable obsession. The minimalist audio, a looping electronic theme (later famously adapted from a Russian folk song), became as iconic as the gameplay itself.

Tetris also introduced subtle psychological principles that designers would study for decades. The increasing speed created a state of "flow," where players were entirely absorbed, losing track of time. The simplicity of the rules, combined with infinite complexity from random sequences, triggered a near-universal compulsion. Studies later showed Tetris players exhibiting measurable changes in spatial reasoning and cognitive patterns — an early demonstration of the cognitive impact of video games.

Cheat culture in Tetris was minimal in the early versions, but advanced strategies evolved. Expert players developed algorithms for stacking, anticipating sequences, and creating the elusive

“Tetris” — clearing four lines at once for maximum points. Competitive marathon sessions required memorisation, patience, and rapid hand-eye coordination, with speed levels eventually reaching dizzying rates.

Unlike other 1980s games dominated by score chasing, Tetris introduced a different form of competition: endurance. Who could survive longest as the blocks accelerated? How high could the stack reach? The game’s inherent fairness — each piece obeys the same rules — meant that success depended on skill rather than luck.

Culturally, Tetris became a bridge between East and West during a politically tense era. A simple Soviet puzzle captivated children and adults across continents, proving that the allure of games transcends language, politics, and geography. Its influence permeates modern gaming, inspiring countless puzzle titles and serving as the blueprint for pattern-based gameplay.

From a design standpoint, Tetris is deceptively perfect:

- Minimalist graphics, maximal engagement
- Progressive difficulty through speed increase
- Clear goals with instant feedback
- Cognitive challenge balanced with accessibility

It was the antithesis of spectacle. No lasers, no explosions, no dragons. Yet its hypnotic appeal arguably surpassed anything on the arcade floor.

Every falling piece carried tension. Every rotated block required decision. And every completed line provided that perfect, fleeting reward.

In 1984, Tetris quietly changed the definition of what a video game could be: not a battleground, not an arcade spectacle, not a narrative quest — but a puzzle of infinite depth.

And once you started, there was no escaping. The blocks kept falling.

Chapter Ten – Mario Bros. and the Rise of the Plumbing Hero

By 1983, Nintendo had already established a reputation for arcade hits like Donkey Kong and Donkey Kong Jr., but the company was still refining the characters and gameplay that would define its future. Into this environment arrived Mario Bros., a deceptively simple yet revolutionary title that introduced one of the most enduring duos in gaming history: Mario and Luigi.

Mario was no longer just Jumpman, the heroic carpenter chasing Pauline across construction sites. He had become a professional plumber, navigating a subterranean world of pipes, fireballs, and strange creatures. Luigi, his taller, green-clad brother, was introduced as the second player's character, marking the first true cooperative gameplay in a Mario-centric title. This cooperative/competitive dynamic would influence decades of multiplayer gaming.

The premise was straightforward: clear the sewers of enemies by flipping them on their backs and kicking them off the platforms. The creatures — including Shellcreepers, Sidesteppers, and Fly

Guys — each had distinct movement patterns. Success required timing, pattern recognition, and precise jumps. Unlike Donkey Kong, Mario Bros. focused less on narrative and more on skillful interaction within a closed environment.

What made the game remarkable was its vertical and horizontal interplay. Players could jump between platforms of varying heights, but hazards lurked on every level. Fireballs appeared periodically, bouncing unpredictably across platforms. Pipes weren't just scenery; they served as entry points for enemies and as structural elements that defined the play area. Players had to move strategically, balancing aggression with caution.

The game also introduced the concept of "stomping," a mechanic that would define Mario's identity for years to come. Timing a jump to land on an enemy was critical — early miscalculations led to instant death. Unlike other arcade games of the era, death in Mario Bros. often came from player error rather than random chance, creating a fair but intense learning curve.

Technologically, the arcade hardware allowed fluid animation for multiple characters and enemies simultaneously, a challenge for early 1980s systems. The game used scrolling platforms and varied sprite behavior to create a sense of depth and dynamism. Unlike the single-screen ascent of Donkey Kong, Mario Bros. encouraged lateral movement and constant attention to multiple levels simultaneously, foreshadowing the complexity of later titles like Super Mario Bros..

Cheat culture in Mario Bros. revolved less around codes and more around exploiting enemy behavior and spawn mechanics. Skilled players learned to manipulate Shellcreeper patterns, stacking multiple flips to rack up points before clearing them. Timing fireball interactions could also grant temporary advantages, rewarding memorisation and practice.

Home ports of Mario Bros. appeared on numerous systems, including the Atari 2600,

Commodore 64, and eventually the Nintendo Entertainment System (NES), where the game became a staple of early console libraries. Each port faced limitations — simplified graphics, reduced enemy behaviors — but preserved the core mechanics that made the arcade version addictive.

Culturally, Mario Bros. marked a turning point. It was the first game to cement Mario as a household name, introduce a consistent universe, and encourage multiplayer cooperation in a skill-based, competitive format. The cooperative rivalry between Mario and Luigi would become a recurring theme in games like Super Mario Bros. 3, Mario Kart, and beyond.

The game also exemplified Nintendo's philosophy: simple controls, clear objectives, tight physics, and a high skill ceiling. Players could immediately understand how to play but could spend endless hours mastering enemy patterns, timing, and point maximisation.

From a design perspective, Mario Bros. introduced several enduring concepts:

Cooperative gameplay with simultaneous or alternating turns

Platform-based enemy interaction and environmental hazards

Stomping as a primary mechanic for combat

Structured, high-score-driven arcade loops with escalating difficulty

Though less visually spectacular than Dragon's Lair or as psychologically hypnotic as Tetris, Mario Bros. offered a new kind of engagement: mastery through repeated practice, pattern recognition, and escalating challenge. Its underground sewer world felt alive, full of movement and peril, yet intuitive enough to invite millions into its universe.

In arcades, the cabinet attracted both solo players and pairs, the latter arguing, competing, or laughing together as enemies were flipped and kicked. At home, the ports brought the challenge into living rooms, cementing Mario and Luigi as enduring icons.

Mario Bros. proved that a character-driven world could thrive on pure mechanics, and that cooperation and competition could coexist within the same experience. It bridged the gap between arcade intensity and home console strategy, paving the way for one of the most influential franchises in video game history.

The plumbers' pipes were not just sewers. They were portals to endless possibilities.

And the adventure was just beginning.

Chapter Eleven - Track & Field and the Birth of Button Mashing

By 1983, arcades were overflowing with platformers, shooters, and maze games, but one genre remained relatively untouched: the sports simulator. Enter Track & Field, Konami's revolutionary take on Olympic-style events. It wasn't about narrative or exploration — it was about pure physicality, reflexes, and endurance.

Track & Field placed players in a series of timed events, from the 100-meter sprint and long jump to javelin and hammer throw. Each event required rapid, precise button presses. Players used two buttons alternately to simulate running, and additional buttons for jumping or throwing. Success depended on the player's stamina, coordination, and willingness to push their fingers to the limit. The sensation of physical exertion transferred from real athletes to arcade-goers, making the game immersive in a surprisingly literal way.

What made Track & Field extraordinary was its design philosophy: intuitive yet punishing. Every event had a simple goal, but achieving the maximum score required understanding the game's mechanics in depth. Sprinting faster meant mastering the rhythm of alternating button presses. Jumping farther required timing the jump at the precise moment of acceleration. Even the javelin demanded understanding trajectory physics, as distance depended on both the speed and the release timing.

The cabinet itself encouraged competition. Two-player machines became arenas for finger-fighting duels, with crowds often gathering to watch intense races and record-breaking attempts. The attract mode featured exaggerated animations of athletes triumphing over opponents, reinforcing the thrill of human achievement.

Technologically, Track & Field pushed arcade hardware to handle multiple simultaneous inputs and responsive sprite animations. The athletes moved smoothly, their limbs responding directly to player input, providing a visceral feedback loop that few games before had achieved. Sound effects — the pounding footsteps, the whoosh of the javelin, the cheering crowds — amplified the sensory intensity.

Home ports, particularly on the Nintendo Entertainment System, captured the essence but faced limitations. The NES controller's smaller button layout made extreme button-mashing more difficult and led to creative alternatives like the infamous "clutch running" techniques, where players tapped or rocked the controller in unconventional ways to gain speed. The difficulty was adjusted for home play, but the core concept — physical exertion translated into game mechanics — remained.

Track & Field popularized several key gaming concepts:

Event-based mini-games forming a larger competitive loop

Skill differentiation based on player input intensity and timing

Physical interaction as a core mechanic, not just cognitive challenge

Direct head-to-head multiplayer competition

Interestingly, Track & Field also created its own "cheat culture." Players experimented with fingers, palms, or even mechanical aids to achieve maximum speed in sprints. High-score enthusiasts memorized event patterns to optimise timing for jumps and throws, turning what seemed like chaotic button-mashing into precise, almost mathematical routines.

Culturally, the game tapped into the 1980s obsession with athletics, competition, and the Olympics. Its visuals evoked international sporting events, while its accessibility meant anyone could attempt to become a champion — at least in pixelated form. Crowds loved it. Players loved it. And operators loved the coins it generated.

From a design perspective, Track & Field proved that simplicity could drive engagement. There was no story, no hero to save, no alien invasion — only human movement distilled into mechanical challenge. Yet that simplicity amplified the thrill. Every sprint, jump, and throw demanded focus, endurance, and precision.

By emphasizing repetition, mastery, and physical interaction, Track & Field influenced countless sports and party games throughout the decade, from later Olympic arcade releases to multiplayer console titles. It proved that gameplay could be both competitive and physically immersive, even on a digital plane.

The whistle blew. The track glowed. Fingers pounded furiously. Every second counted.

In 1983, arcade athletes were born — and their battles would echo across arcades and living rooms for years to come.

Chapter Twelve – Ghosts 'n Goblins and the Art of Punishing Courage

By 1985, arcades were crowded with bright, inviting titles, yet one game dared to be brutally unforgiving. Ghosts 'n Goblins, developed by Capcom, combined horror, platforming, and relentless difficulty to create an experience that would haunt players' memories — and their thumbs — for decades.

You played as Sir Arthur, a knight in shining armor, tasked with rescuing Princess Prin-Prin from the clutches of demons, zombies, and grotesque creatures. From the first screen, the game made its intentions clear: failure was inevitable, death was constant, and only perseverance would triumph. Every jump, every shot, every timing decision mattered.

What set Ghosts 'n Goblins apart was its dual-layered challenge. First, the enemies themselves were relentless. Skeletons moved in unpredictable patterns, zombies shambled with deceptive speed, and demons could appear from unexpected corners or descend from the sky. Every collision with an enemy, no matter how slight, removed one layer of Arthur's armor, leaving him vulnerable in his iconic underwear — a visual punishment that became a defining image of the franchise.

Second, the level design was merciless. Platforms were narrow, jumps precise, and hazards abound. Fireballs, pitfalls, and moving obstacles required precise timing. Even the layout of power-ups and weapons encouraged calculated risk, tempting players into danger for a chance at survival.

The game also introduced weapon variety. Arthur could wield lances, knives, axes, and torches, each with distinct patterns and ranges. Choosing the right weapon for each encounter became a matter of strategy. Certain weapons allowed easier handling of flying enemies, while others excelled against ground-based foes. Mastery required both skill and knowledge of the levels' intricate design.

Technologically, Ghosts 'n Goblins pushed arcade hardware to its limits. Sprites were detailed, with fluid animation despite numerous enemies appearing simultaneously. The parallax scrolling backgrounds created depth, giving the illusion of a more expansive, layered world than the arcade screen could naturally display. Sound design — the clanging of Arthur's armor, the screeches of monsters, and the iconic haunting music — reinforced tension and urgency.

Cheat culture arose out of necessity. Players discovered patterns for enemy movement and level layout to minimise risk, often memorising sequences to survive longer. Some exploited jumps and weapon quirks to bypass particularly lethal sections. Yet the core challenge — surviving the relentless pace and recovering from errors — remained, making true mastery extremely difficult.

Home ports appeared on multiple platforms, including the Nintendo Entertainment System, Commodore 64, and Amiga. While the NES version faithfully recreated the arcade challenge, memory limitations and control responsiveness sometimes made certain sections even more punishing.

Despite this, it became a cult favorite, defining the concept of "hardcore" gaming for home consoles.

Culturally, Ghosts 'n Goblins established several conventions that would echo in gaming for decades:

Extreme difficulty as a deliberate design choice

Visual representation of player vulnerability (armor loss)

Layered environmental hazards requiring timing and planning

Pattern memorisation as a core skill

The game's punishing nature was not universally loved, yet it instilled a sense of accomplishment unmatched by easier contemporaries. Completing even a single loop of the game was considered an extraordinary feat. Ghosts 'n Goblins did not reward casual play. It demanded focus, practice, and patience.

From a design perspective, it demonstrated that high difficulty could be engaging when paired with clear rules and consistent feedback. Every death taught the player something about enemy behavior, level layout, or timing. The frustration was balanced by a clear path to mastery.

The horror aesthetic, combined with medieval heroism, also set a precedent. Many later games — from the Castlevania series to modern action-platformers — drew inspiration from its blend of gothic environments, relentless enemies, and rewarding skill-based progression.

In the arcades, Ghosts 'n Goblins drew crowds equally fascinated and terrified by its difficulty. Friends would gather to watch each attempt, gasp at near-misses, and celebrate rare triumphs. At home, the NES ports turned living rooms into arenas of perseverance, where repeated failure was a badge of honor.

Sir Arthur's armor gleamed. Monsters swarmed. Each misstep was a lesson. And each victory, however brief, felt monumental.

In 1985, Ghosts 'n Goblins reminded the gaming world that courage alone was never enough. Only skill, timing, and relentless persistence could save the day — and even then, the journey would loop again.

Chapter Thirteen - Commando and the Birth of Run-and-Gun Warfare

By 1985, arcade cabinets had grown increasingly sophisticated, but few titles captured the intensity of modern combat like Commando. Developed by Capcom, Commando was a vertically scrolling run-and-gun shooter that placed players directly into the boots of a lone soldier facing overwhelming enemy forces. Its blend of speed, strategy, and relentless firepower would influence an entire generation of military-themed games.

Players controlled Super Joe, a single soldier dropped behind enemy lines, armed with a rifle and grenades. Unlike earlier shooters such as Galaga, Commando did not confine action to a single screen. The map scrolled vertically, presenting waves of enemies, barricades, and gun emplacements. Players had to move constantly, dodging fire while advancing through forests, deserts, and enemy compounds. Survival demanded reflexes, positioning, and tactical awareness.

Enemy design was both diverse and unforgiving. Foot soldiers charged with machine guns, soldiers threw grenades, and turrets required careful timing to neutralize. Some enemies could absorb multiple hits, while others swarmed in coordinated patterns. Each level presented a delicate balance: too aggressive, and the player would be overwhelmed; too cautious, and progress would stall, leaving the screen filled with approaching adversaries.

What set Commando apart was its dual-layered strategy. While quick reflexes were critical, map awareness and prioritization of threats were equally important. Players could shoot enemies at range, throw grenades for area damage, or even bait foes into traps. Deciding whether to focus on advancing or cleaning the screen was a constant tactical consideration, giving the game a depth that belied its simple premise.

Technologically, Commando pushed arcade hardware to handle large numbers of moving sprites and smooth vertical scrolling. Each enemy had programmed behaviors, allowing patterns that were predictable yet challenging. Sound design reinforced tension — rapid gunfire, grenade explosions, and distant alarms created a chaotic battlefield atmosphere. The visual cues, from smoke trails to enemy flashes, allowed attentive players to anticipate attacks and survive longer.

Cheat culture emerged organically. Advanced players memorized enemy spawn patterns and developed precise movement paths to avoid damage while maximizing efficiency. Grenade placement became an art form; timing a throw perfectly could wipe out multiple enemies in one stroke, conserving lives and creating high-score opportunities. Unlike many arcade games, Commando rewarded not just reflexes but strategy and memorization.

Home ports of Commando appeared on systems like the Commodore 64, ZX Spectrum, and NES. While hardware limitations required some compromises — reduced enemy counts, slower scrolling, and simplified graphics — the core gameplay survived intact. The NES version, in particular, translated the intensity well, with tight controls and faithful level design, making it a popular title for home players seeking the arcade thrill without leaving their living rooms.

Culturally, Commando tapped into the 1980s fascination with military adventure and elite soldiers. The Cold War era, action films, and comics all reinforced the appeal of a lone hero taking on impossible odds. The game's relentless pace and high difficulty made it both a challenge and a spectacle. Friends crowded around cabinets to watch skilled players advance further than anyone expected, celebrating clever grenade throws or near-death escapes.

From a design standpoint, Commando introduced several enduring mechanics:

Vertical scrolling maps for continuous progression

Multiple attack options (rifle, grenades) for tactical choice

Enemy waves with predictable yet challenging patterns

High-score incentive tied to survival and efficiency

Commando also popularized the "run-and-gun" genre, inspiring successors such as Ikari Warriors, Contra, and Metal Slug. Its combination of speed, strategy, and risk-reward gameplay became a template for decades of military-themed arcade and console shooters.

Every screen demanded attention. Every grenade counted. Every shot carried the potential to save or end the mission.

In 1985, Commando reminded players that the battlefield was unforgiving, but mastery — careful observation, quick reflexes, and precise planning — could allow one lone soldier to conquer overwhelming odds.

The battlefield was endless. The enemy relentless. And for the player willing to endure, glory awaited — one coin at a time.

Chapter Fourteen - Gradius and the Birth of Strategic Shooting

By 1985, arcades were saturated with shooters, yet few games combined reflexive action with strategic depth like Gradius. Developed by Konami, Gradius was a side-scrolling space shooter that transformed the genre, introducing a customizable power-up system, memorable enemy design, and a pacing structure that required both quick reflexes and forward planning.

Players controlled the Vic Viper, a sleek spacecraft tasked with navigating hostile alien environments while fending off waves of enemies, projectiles, and environmental hazards. Unlike the simplistic shooters of earlier years, Gradius demanded situational awareness. The screen scrolled continuously to the right, forcing players to move forward while dodging bullets, mines, and multi-part bosses. Retreat was impossible; the challenge was relentless and unforgiving.

Gradius introduced one of its most revolutionary mechanics: the power-up bar. Rather than collecting a single item for a predetermined upgrade, players accrued capsules that allowed them to choose upgrades — speed boosts, missiles, double shots, lasers, and shields. Strategic selection became as important as reflexes. Do you speed up to dodge bullets more easily, or invest in missiles to deal with tougher enemies? The system encouraged planning and adaptation, adding layers of depth to what could have been a simple shoot-em-up.

Enemy design in Gradius was methodical yet diverse. The formations were patterned but deadly, with coordinated attacks that required memorization and precise movement. Environmental hazards such as indestructible barriers, turrets, and moving obstacles created additional tension. Boss encounters were elaborate, often multi-stage battles demanding mastery of both movement and power-up strategy. Unlike many arcade shooters, where success depended solely on dodging bullets, Gradius required foresight and resource management.

The game also introduced checkpoint-based progression. Unlike endless shooters, death in

Gradius often meant restarting from a nearby checkpoint rather than the beginning. This allowed players to tackle complex stages without total frustration, while still punishing mistakes enough to maintain tension. The balance between accessibility and challenge became a hallmark of the series.

Technologically, Gradius pushed the arcade hardware of the time. It handled multiple scrolling layers, dynamic sprite animation, and a variety of enemy patterns simultaneously. The game's visuals — industrial alien landscapes, starfields, and dramatic explosions — created a sense of immersion that few contemporaries matched. Its music, composed by Miki Higashino, provided rhythmic cues that reinforced the pacing of the action, heightening the tension and urgency of each stage.

Cheat and strategy culture emerged quickly. Expert players learned optimal power-up paths, memorized enemy patterns, and timed weapon upgrades to maximize efficiency. Knowing when to deploy missiles, lasers, or shields could be the difference between survival and instant death. High-score mastery required not only dexterity but strategic thinking, making Gradius a favorite among competitive arcade enthusiasts.

Home ports of Gradius appeared on the Nintendo Entertainment System, MSX computers, and numerous 8-bit systems. While hardware limitations forced some compromises — simpler graphics, fewer enemies on-screen — the core power-up mechanics and side-scrolling intensity survived. On the NES, Gradius introduced many players to the concept of layered, strategic shooting in a home setting, setting the stage for sequels, spin-offs, and the broader “shoot-em-up” genre.

Culturally, Gradius represented a shift in arcade design philosophy: it rewarded planning, adaptability, and mastery rather than brute force or rapid reflexes alone. Its combination of continuous scrolling, customizable upgrades, and elaborate level design influenced a generation of developers, inspiring classics like R-Type, Salamander, and even later entries in the modern bullet-hell genre.

From a design perspective, Gradius introduced several enduring innovations:

Strategic power-up selection and resource management

Checkpoint-based level progression to balance challenge and fairness

Multi-layered side-scrolling environments with patterned enemies

Complex, multi-stage boss encounters requiring both skill and strategy

Every stage tested not only reflexes but foresight. Every power-up choice influenced survival. Every death was a lesson in timing, positioning, and strategy.

In 1985, Gradius proved that a shooter could be more than mindless destruction — it could be a carefully balanced dance of reflex, planning, and risk-reward decision-making. The stars themselves became the battlefield, and only the prepared pilot would survive the relentless onslaught of the Vic Viper's enemies.

Chapter Fifteen - Gauntlet and the Rise of Cooperative Dungeon Crawling

By 1985, the arcade world was dominated by shooters, platformers, and puzzle games, yet few titles offered a true cooperative experience that combined exploration, combat, and strategy. Gauntlet, developed by Atari Games, did exactly that. It transformed the arcade into a dungeon, the players into heroes, and the coins they inserted into tickets of survival, teamwork, and endless replayability.

Gauntlet's premise was deceptively simple: players chose a character class — Warrior, Valkyrie, Wizard, or Elf — and descended into labyrinthine dungeons filled with hordes of monsters, deadly traps, and treasure. Each class had unique attributes: the Warrior was durable and strong, the Valkyrie balanced speed and defense, the Wizard was fragile but wielded powerful magic, and the Elf offered speed and ranged attacks. This diversity encouraged cooperative play, as each character's strengths complemented the others.

The game's top-down, multi-screen dungeon design was innovative. Unlike linear side-scrolling adventures, Gauntlet's levels twisted and turned, with hidden corridors, locked doors, and secret rooms. Players had to navigate mazes while managing health, ammunition, and enemy aggression. The simplicity of the interface — an attack button and movement joystick — belied the depth of strategic decisions required to survive.

Enemies were relentless. Skeletons, trolls, fireballs, and more swarmed the players in waves. Health was finite, and each hit drained a portion of the player's life. In true arcade fashion, extra lives could be earned through coin insertions or by discovering hidden items, but death was ever-present, a constant reminder of the dungeon's danger. The famous "wizard scream" — a digitized voice exclaiming "Wizard needs food, badly!" — became an iconic audio cue that added urgency and personality to the otherwise tense dungeon crawl.

The arcade cabinet supported up to four players simultaneously, creating a dynamic of collaboration and chaos. Players could strategize

— focusing attacks on bosses, covering retreat paths, or dividing to collect treasures — or compete, as grabbing items sometimes meant denying them to others. The chaos of multiple players on one screen, combined with endless enemy hordes, made Gauntlet one of the first true social arcade experiences, paving the way for multiplayer-centric games of the late 80s and 90s.

Technologically, Gauntlet handled large numbers of sprites, responsive input for multiple players, and procedural enemy spawns that ensured the dungeons felt alive. Sound design played a critical role: the clanging of swords, the firing of spells, the groans of monsters, and the constant background music heightened tension and immersion. The digital voice samples were revolutionary for the time, adding character and urgency to the gameplay.

Cheat culture quickly emerged among dedicated players. Exploiting enemy spawn patterns, sharing class-specific strategies, or intentionally losing health to manipulate item spawns became common tactics. Memorization of dungeon layouts allowed advanced players to plan efficient paths, collect treasures, and avoid ambushes. Unlike many arcade games that emphasized reflexes alone, Gauntlet rewarded both quick thinking and tactical planning.

Home ports appeared on systems such as the Commodore 64, Atari 7800, and later the NES. While early ports had to simplify graphics and reduce the number of simultaneous players due to hardware limitations, the core cooperative gameplay survived. Gauntlet became a template for dungeon crawlers on home consoles and PCs, influencing later classics such as Diablo, Baldur's Gate: Dark Alliance, and Gauntlet: Dark Legacy.

Culturally, Gauntlet introduced many players to cooperative gameplay in a high-stakes environment. It created memorable social interactions, from the tension of sharing scarce resources to the exhilaration of defeating overwhelming enemy hordes together. The mix of action, strategy, and teamwork resonated with a broad audience, helping to popularize multiplayer-focused arcade experiences.

From a design standpoint, Gauntlet pioneered several enduring concepts:

Cooperative multiplayer with distinct character classes

Top-down dungeon navigation with exploration and combat integration

Resource management (health, ammo, power-ups)

Procedural enemy spawns combined with strategic level design

Every corridor held danger. Every monster required attention. Every coin inserted fueled survival — or failure.

In 1985, Gauntlet redefined what an arcade could be: not merely a place for solo reflex testing, but a shared battlefield of monsters, treasures, and strategy. Four heroes could descend into the labyrinth together, survive the chaos, and emerge victorious — or perish in spectacular, chaotic fashion.

The dungeons waited. Monsters lurked. And every player's choice mattered.

Chapter Sixteen – Rampage and the Joy of Destruction

By 1986, arcade games were exploring new frontiers: cooperative play, innovative mechanics, and experiences that broke away from traditional shooting or platforming. Rampage, developed by Bally Midway, embraced one of the purest forms of fun — destruction. Players became gigantic monsters, leveling cities, smashing buildings, and wreaking havoc on a scale previously unimaginable in video games.

The premise was simple but exhilarating. Players controlled one of three massive monsters — George, a mutated ape; Lizzie, a giant lizard; and Ralph, a towering werewolf — and proceeded to climb skyscrapers, punch walls, eat civilians, and dodge military forces. Each city was a playground of chaos. Tanks, helicopters, and soldiers attempted to stop the monsters, but the sheer size and power of the creatures made the destruction feel almost cathartic.

What made Rampage unique was its cooperative and competitive dynamic. Up to three players could play simultaneously, climbing buildings together, competing for points, or simply collaborating to obliterate every structure in sight. The arcade cabinet itself encouraged social play — players could brawl monsters against each other while still enjoying cooperative city-wide destruction. The chaos was a spectacle; the joy of breaking things was immediate and universally understood.

The gameplay was deceptively deep. Each building required multiple hits to destroy, but players had to avoid projectiles, falling debris, and the occasional special attack. Civilians provided bonus points but could also trigger hazards if mishandled. Timing, positioning, and coordination between players determined not just survival, but high-score success. Advanced players learned to manipulate enemy patterns, maximize destruction in a limited time, and coordinate jumps and attacks to keep combos going.

Technologically, Rampage leveraged hardware to create multiple large sprites moving independently across the screen, a challenge at the time. Buildings crumbled in stages, requiring smooth animation for collapsing walls and debris. The sound design amplified the chaotic experience: smashing, roaring, and screaming civilians combined with explosive sound effects created an immersive sense of power and mayhem.

Cheat and strategy culture arose organically. High-score enthusiasts memorized patterns of enemy attacks, optimized movement paths for maximum building destruction, and coordinated with other players for combo bonuses. Some players discovered tricks to repeatedly trigger hidden points by manipulating civilians or exploiting physics quirks in collapsing structures. While simple at first glance, Rampage rewarded both coordination and mastery of timing.

Home ports followed on platforms like the Commodore 64, NES, and later handheld systems. Naturally, the home versions could not fully replicate the arcade's spectacle: sprite limits, smaller screens, and reduced simultaneous character count softened the chaos. Yet the core appeal — the fantasy of playing a massive, unstoppable monster — survived intact, introducing home audiences to the thrill of controlled destruction.

Culturally, Rampage tapped into a universal thrill: the joy of smashing things without consequence. The 1980s were full of blockbuster monster films like Godzilla and King Kong, and Rampage captured that same adrenaline in interactive form. The cooperative chaos also made it a social phenomenon; arcades were filled with laughter, shouting, and cheering as players toppled entire cityscapes in minutes.

From a design perspective, Rampage established enduring concepts:

Large, player-controlled destructive characters as central gameplay

Cooperative and competitive multiplayer in the same experience

Environmental interaction as both obstacle and scoring mechanism

Immediate, cathartic feedback from player actions

Every building climbed. Every wall smashed. Every tank destroyed reinforced the exhilaration of power. Rampage didn't require strategy in the conventional sense; it demanded presence, coordination, and a willingness to embrace chaos.

In 1986, Rampage proved that sometimes the most compelling gameplay is about letting go — tearing down walls, stomping tanks, and reveling in the sheer thrill of destruction. The monsters roared. The cities fell. And the players laughed, united by chaos, destruction, and a timeless arcade joy.

Chapter Seventeen - Out Run and the Thrill of the Open Road

By 1986, the arcade landscape had begun embracing not just action or shooting, but experiences that simulated freedom, speed, and exhilaration. Out Run, developed by Sega and designed by Yu Suzuki, became the definitive driving experience of the 1980s, marrying technical innovation with pure, unadulterated fun.

Out Run put players behind the wheel of a red Ferrari Testarossa Spider, accelerating down sun-soaked highways, winding coastal roads, and scenic countrysides. Unlike conventional racing games that emphasized lap times or head-to-head competition, Out Run was about the journey itself — freedom of choice, risk-taking, and the thrill of speed. Its branching paths allowed players to steer into different routes at the end of each stage, providing multiple endings and encouraging repeated playthroughs to discover all possible courses.

The controls were intuitive yet precise. Players used a steering wheel, accelerator, and brake pedal, complemented by a gear shift for high-speed nuance. Success required balancing speed, cornering, and lane positioning while navigating traffic, sharp turns, and environmental hazards like cliffs or bridges. The sense of velocity was amplified by a pseudo-3D sprite-scaling system that made the road appear to rush past the player, a visual feat remarkable for mid-1980s hardware.

Out Run's design was as much about sensory experience as gameplay. The soundtrack, selectable from multiple tracks, provided an energetic, synth-driven backdrop that perfectly complemented the sensation of cruising through endless, stylized landscapes. Visuals ranged from palm-lined boulevards to snowy mountains, with bright, colorful sprites, dynamic scenery, and a parallax effect that created depth and immersion. Every detail — the car's shifting reflections, roadside obstacles, and other vehicles — contributed to a believable and thrilling sense of speed.

Arcade cabinets themselves were part of the magic. Some featured hydraulic motion, vibrating in response to turns, crashes, and acceleration, creating a physical sensation of driving. The combination of responsive controls, motion feedback, and immersive audio made Out Run a multi-sensory experience that few games of the era could match.

Cheat culture and advanced techniques quickly emerged. Expert players memorized branching routes to optimize times, learned subtle braking and cornering tricks to maintain speed, and discovered patterns in AI-controlled traffic to avoid collisions. Mastery of the game often required both skillful handling and strategic route selection, rewarding those willing to invest the time to explore its mechanics fully.

Home ports were developed for systems including the Sega Master System, Commodore 64, and later the NES. While hardware limitations meant simplified graphics and reduced sprite scaling, the essence of speed, branching paths, and soundtrack selection survived. Home versions allowed players to bring the exhilaration of arcade racing into their living rooms, cultivating a generation fascinated by driving games.

Culturally, Out Run captured the essence of 1980s optimism, adventure, and escapism. The bright, stylized environments, carefree music, and high-speed thrills embodied the decade's love for freedom, style, and the open road. Arcades became a stage for friends to compete for the fastest times or simply enjoy the sheer joy of a virtual road trip.

From a design perspective, Out Run introduced several enduring innovations:

Branching pathways that encouraged exploration and replayability

Pseudo-3D sprite scaling for realistic speed perception

Immersive audio integrated into gameplay choice

Multi-sensory cabinet experiences with motion and feedback

Every turn demanded attention. Every branching road promised new vistas. Every acceleration offered the intoxicating taste of speed. Out Run was less about winning and more about the journey — a concept rare in 1980s arcades but perfectly executed here.

In 1986, Out Run demonstrated that a game could simulate not just challenge, but joy, freedom, and pure adrenaline. The engine roared. The road stretched ahead. And for a few precious minutes, players could escape reality and lose themselves in the open road.

Chapter Eighteen - Paperboy and the Chaos of Suburban Delivery

By 1985, arcade games were experimenting with new settings, unconventional heroes, and gameplay that broke away from traditional combat or racing. Paperboy, developed by Atari Games, turned a mundane suburban occupation — newspaper delivery — into a tense, action-packed arcade experience. What made Paperboy remarkable wasn't its premise but the way it combined timing, precision, and environmental interaction into an addictive, high-score-driven challenge.

Players assumed the role of the titular paperboy, pedaling through a suburban neighborhood on a bicycle while tossing newspapers to customers' homes. At first glance, it seemed simple: deliver papers to subscribers and avoid obstacles. But the streets were alive with danger. Lawn mowers, cars, dogs, skateboarders, bouncing balls, and even unruly kids created a dynamic, unpredictable environment. Every delivery required timing, aim, and situational awareness. A misthrown paper could cost points, while a collision could end the player's run prematurely.

The game's perspective was isometric, giving players a three-dimensional sense of depth as they navigated streets and alleys. This design allowed for precise targeting, but also meant that judging distances and trajectories was a constant challenge. Players had to learn the subtleties of the paper toss: angle, speed, and timing mattered, especially when aiming for mailboxes or moving targets. Each successful delivery rewarded points, while mistakes triggered feedback in the form of damaged houses, angry customers, or lost papers.

Environmental hazards were not merely obstacles; they were interactive elements that defined the gameplay loop. Breaking a neighbor's window, running over a flowerpot, or colliding with traffic didn't just punish the player — it added chaos, increased the challenge, and created a memorable sense of consequence. Mastery of Paperboy required memorization of hazards, precise maneuvering, and strategic planning to maximize deliveries while avoiding disaster.

Technologically, Paperboy pushed 1980s arcade hardware with its smooth scrolling streets, animated pedestrians, and responsive bicycle controls. The game's audio cues — the jingling of papers, dogs barking, car horns, and shouts from angry residents — enhanced immersion and urgency. Each week's route became progressively more difficult, with new hazards introduced and speed increased, keeping players constantly on edge.

Cheat culture and advanced strategies quickly emerged. Skilled players memorized routes, optimizing paper throws and bike positioning to maximize points. Some discovered that targeting specific objects could create chain reactions, multiplying their score. Perfect runs required precise timing and a thorough understanding of each neighborhood's quirks.

Home ports for the Nintendo Entertainment System, Atari 7800, Commodore 64, and even home computers allowed players to bring the suburban chaos into their living rooms. While early ports simplified some hazards and reduced frame rates, the core mechanics — navigation, aiming, and obstacle management — remained intact, preserving the game's tense and addictive feel.

Culturally, Paperboy captured the charm and absurdity of suburban life in a way no other arcade game had. The combination of ordinary settings, interactive hazards, and an unconventional hero resonated with players. It also introduced humor and whimsy into arcades, contrasting with the often intense or violent themes of the era. Watching a player narrowly avoid a mailbox crash or a dog attack became entertainment in itself, fostering both competitive high-score culture and casual amusement.

From a design perspective, Paperboy introduced enduring concepts:

Isometric perspective for precise depth perception and navigation

Environmental hazards as both obstacle and interactive gameplay element

Timing-based mechanics combined with strategy and memorization

High-score-driven progression rewarding mastery and risk-taking

Every street held danger. Every delivery demanded focus. Every misthrown paper reminded players that even mundane tasks could be thrilling in the hands of skilled designers.

In 1985, Paperboy transformed the ordinary into the extraordinary. It demonstrated that arcade excitement didn't require epic battles or high-speed chases — sometimes, all it took was a bicycle, a handful of newspapers, and a chaotic suburban neighborhood.

The bells jingled. Dogs barked. Mailboxes trembled. And the paperboy pedaled on, determined to survive the week and deliver every last newspaper.

Chapter Nineteen - Arkanoid and the Evolution of Breakout

By 1986, video games were beginning to experiment with reinventing classic concepts, and few transformations were as successful as Arkanoid, developed by Taito. Taking inspiration from Atari's 1976 Breakout, Arkanoid elevated the simple paddle-and-ball gameplay into a sophisticated, visually striking, and strategically rich arcade experience that would captivate players for years.

Players controlled the Vaus, a small paddle-shaped spacecraft at the bottom of the screen, tasked with bouncing a ball to destroy arrays of colored bricks above. While the concept was familiar, Arkanoid introduced new mechanics that added depth, challenge, and excitement. Power-ups occasionally fell from broken bricks, offering advantages such as laser cannons, multiple balls, extended paddle width, or "catch" abilities that allowed the ball to stick to the paddle temporarily. These additions transformed a simple reflex-based game into one requiring planning, timing, and adaptability.

Levels were intricately designed, with bricks arranged in patterns that challenged both precision and strategy. Some bricks were indestructible, forcing players to navigate around them and anticipate ball trajectories. As stages progressed, ball speed increased and patterns became more complex, requiring careful calculation and quick reflexes. The game's difficulty curve was expertly tuned, ensuring that beginners could enjoy early stages while veteran players were tested to their limits by advanced levels.

Enemy elements further enriched the gameplay. Certain bricks released capsules with power-ups or hazards, while occasional enemies appeared that could interfere with ball movement. Some power-ups even had mixed effects — a seemingly helpful capsule could shrink the paddle or speed up the ball, introducing a calculated risk that added tension and excitement. The combination of rewards, hazards, and strategic paddle positioning created a rhythm that demanded both skill and attention.

Technologically, Arkanoid was impressive for its time. Smooth scrolling, fluid ball physics, responsive controls, and colorful, animated brick designs created an engaging audiovisual experience. Sound effects punctuated each collision, providing immediate feedback that reinforced timing and precision. The visuals, with their bright colors and dynamic stage layouts, made each level feel alive and purposeful, while the increasing ball speed and complex patterns ensured constant engagement.

Cheat culture and advanced strategies emerged quickly. Expert players memorized brick layouts and power-up sequences, optimizing paddle movement and ball angles for maximum efficiency. Learning to anticipate multiple bounces, chain reactions, and the effects of temporary power-ups became essential for high-score mastery. The game rewarded precision, timing, and foresight, turning what could have been a simple casual experience into a demanding, skill-based challenge.

Home ports were released for the Nintendo Entertainment System, Commodore 64, MSX, and various other platforms. While home systems sometimes simplified graphics or reduced power-up variety, the core gameplay survived intact. Arkanoid's success in arcades translated to living rooms, introducing players to precise control mechanics and strategic timing that influenced countless puzzle and action titles in the years to come.

Culturally, Arkanoid represented the refinement of arcade design: taking a simple, proven idea and layering depth, challenge, and aesthetic polish to create a timeless experience. It bridged generations of players, offering familiarity to fans of Breakout while introducing new strategic complexity. Competitive high-score culture flourished, with players seeking to complete stages flawlessly and maximize point totals.

From a design perspective, Arkanoid established enduring concepts:

Power-up systems that modify core mechanics dynamically

Increasing difficulty curves balanced with accessibility

Environmental and enemy interactions integrated with core gameplay

Precision-based challenge rewarding both reflex and strategy

Every bounce mattered. Every power-up was a potential advantage or hazard. Every miscalculated angle could undo minutes of effort.

In 1986, Arkanoid proved that reinvention could elevate a simple concept into an iconic experience. It demonstrated that mastery, strategy, and reflexes could coexist in a deceptively simple game, turning a paddle and ball into a vehicle for skill, challenge, and timeless arcade enjoyment.

The ball flew. Bricks shattered. The Vaus glided across the screen. And players learned that even the simplest tools, wielded with skill, could conquer complexity.

Chapter Twenty - Street Fighter II and the Birth of the Fighting Game Revolution

By 1991, the arcade scene was primed for innovation, but few titles would redefine competitive gaming like Street Fighter II, developed by Capcom. Building on the foundation of the original Street Fighter (1987), which introduced one-on-one combat in a fighting arena, Street Fighter II exploded into the mainstream by combining precise mechanics, memorable characters, and deep strategy — transforming fighting games from a novelty into a cultural phenomenon.

Players selected from a roster of diverse fighters, each with unique abilities, fighting styles, and special moves. Ryu, the disciplined karateka; Ken, his fiery American counterpart; Chun-Li, the agile Chinese martial artist; Guile, the disciplined American soldier — these were just a few of the characters whose personalities, nationalities, and signature moves created an instantly recognizable world of combat. Each character required mastery of timing, spacing, and combo execution, making the game both accessible to beginners and rewarding for experts.

The gameplay was deceptively simple on the surface: two characters faced each other in a best-of-three round match, depleting the opponent's health bar with punches, kicks, and special moves. But beneath this simplicity lay a system of intricate mechanics. Special moves required precise directional inputs combined with button presses, a design choice that introduced skill expression, risk-reward decision-making, and strategic mind games between players. Combos — sequences of attacks strung together — became essential tools for advanced play, giving players the ability to turn a single opening into devastating damage.

Street Fighter II also introduced a variety of game modes and innovations. The arcade version supported competitive two-player matches, igniting rivalries in arcades across the globe. Single-player mode featured battles against CPU-controlled characters, culminating in increasingly difficult fights against the game's boss characters, including M. Bison, Balrog, Vega, and Sagat. Each opponent had distinct behaviors and attack patterns, teaching players to adapt and anticipate while maintaining their own offensive and defensive strategy.

Technologically, Street Fighter II pushed the limits of arcade hardware. Detailed sprite animation, vibrant stages representing different countries, and expressive character portraits brought fighters to life. The fluid animations allowed for readable attack telegraphs, which were crucial for competitive play. Sound design also played a key role: character grunts, voice samples, and signature move sounds provided both feedback and personality, while dynamic music tracks underscored the tension and excitement of each battle.

Cheat culture and expert strategies flourished. Players developed intricate knowledge of frame data, hitboxes, and move priority — concepts that would later become fundamental in competitive fighting games. Combos were discovered and perfected, exploiting timing windows to maximize damage. Tournament culture began emerging organically in arcades, as groups of friends and strangers alike gathered to test skill, refine techniques, and engage in intense rivalries. Street Fighter II effectively transformed the arcade into a proving ground for competitive skill.

Home ports brought Street Fighter II into living rooms via systems like the Super Nintendo Entertainment System, Sega Genesis, and later PC platforms. These ports captured much of the arcade's speed and complexity, enabling players to experience both single-player campaigns and head-to-head battles at home. The accessibility of home versions expanded the game's cultural impact, turning competitive fighting into a mainstream pastime and laying the foundation for modern esports.

Culturally, Street Fighter II was revolutionary. It elevated fighting games into a social experience, inspiring tournaments, arcade rivalries, and even a surge in martial arts popularity. Its characters became iconic symbols, influencing animation, comics, toys, and other media. The game's emphasis on skill, timing, and strategy reshaped how designers approached multiplayer competition, inspiring countless sequels, spin-offs, and the broader fighting game genre.

From a design standpoint, Street Fighter II introduced several enduring innovations:

Character diversity with unique abilities and national identities

Deep input mechanics enabling skill expression through timing and combos

Balanced risk-reward design for strategic offensive and defensive play

Competitive two-player arcade matches as a social and cultural phenomenon

Every fight demanded attention. Every special move required precision. Every victory and defeat was a lesson in timing, strategy, and adaptability.

In 1991, Street Fighter II redefined what a fighting game could be. It turned arcades into battlegrounds, homes into training arenas, and casual players into competitors. Its legacy — from combo mastery to tournament culture — continues to shape gaming decades later.

The crowd roared. Fists flew. Fireballs streaked across the screen. And players learned that in the world of Street Fighter II, skill, patience, and heart determined the true champion.

Chapter Twenty-One - Pit-Fighter and the Rise of Digitized Combat

By 1990, arcade fighting games had exploded in popularity, and developers were experimenting with new ways to make combat feel more realistic. Pit-Fighter, developed by Atari Games, was a bold experiment in digitized graphics and visceral, chaotic fighting. Unlike the smooth, sprite-based fighters of the era, Pit-Fighter used digitized images of real actors, giving characters a raw, gritty appearance that set the game apart in arcades worldwide.

Players chose from three main fighters: Buzz, a muscular street brawler; Ty, a nimble and balanced fighter; and Kato, a fast, agile martial artist. Each character had unique attacks and strengths, but the core gameplay emphasized aggressive, fast-paced combat rather than intricate combos or strategic zoning. Pit-Fighter's arenas were brutal and unforgiving: dimly lit cages, graffiti-covered rings, and industrial backdrops gave the fights a gritty, underground aesthetic that felt closer to a street brawl than a polished martial arts tournament.

Gameplay revolved around hand-to-hand combat in a single-screen arena. Players could punch, kick, jump, or grapple opponents, combining attacks to inflict damage. Environmental hazards — chains, barrels, and electrified floors in certain stages — added unpredictability, forcing players to adapt their tactics on the fly. Unlike other fighters of the time, Pit-Fighter emphasized raw aggression and chaos, rewarding players who could control the frenetic pace while avoiding damage.

The game's digitized graphics were revolutionary for 1990. Using live actors recorded frame by frame, the developers created characters that moved and reacted with surprising realism, though the animation could be stiff compared to hand-drawn sprites. This technique gave Pit-Fighter a distinct visual identity, making it immediately recognizable in crowded arcades. The combination of digitized fighters and industrial, underground arenas created a visceral atmosphere that was both thrilling and slightly shocking to players used to clean, colorful fighting games.

Cheat and advanced play strategies emerged naturally. Knowledge of hitboxes, grapple timing, and movement patterns allowed players to maximize damage while avoiding counters. Certain stages allowed for creative interactions with the environment, giving skilled players ways to manipulate hazards against opponents. While simpler than the combo-heavy fighters like Street Fighter II, Pit-Fighter demanded timing, positioning, and a keen sense of spacing to dominate the arena.

Arcade culture embraced Pit-Fighter for its novelty and spectacle. Its digitized characters made it stand out visually, while the multiplayer brawls created chaotic, social gameplay. Watching two or three players go at it in a cage arena became a spectator event in itself, with players cheering, shouting advice, and celebrating brutal knockouts. The game's aggressive tone, combined with its realistic appearance, made it one of the most talked-about fighting games of its era.

Home ports appeared on the Super Nintendo Entertainment System, Genesis, and DOS computers. While home versions were limited by hardware — reducing resolution, frame rate, and animation smoothness — they preserved the core digitized aesthetic and fast-paced combat. For many players, these home versions offered the first opportunity to experience the gritty, chaotic fights in their living rooms.

From a design perspective, Pit-Fighter introduced and reinforced several concepts:

Digitized characters for a more “realistic” visual style

Fast, aggressive combat emphasizing reaction and positioning

Interactive environments as both obstacle and tactical tool

Multiplayer arena combat as a chaotic, social spectacle

Every punch mattered. Every grapple could change the outcome. Every environmental hazard added tension and strategy. Pit-Fighter was not elegant or polished — it was raw, chaotic, and exhilarating.

In 1990, Pit-Fighter reminded players that fighting games could be brutal, visceral, and visually groundbreaking. It was a precursor to future digitized brawlers and a milestone in arcade innovation, proving that realism, chaos, and multiplayer fun could coexist in a single cage.

The fighters lunged. The crowd roared. And in every cage, victory was earned through aggression, timing, and nerves of steel.

Chapter Twenty-Two – Teenage Mutant Ninja Turtles: The Arcade Game and the Beat-'Em-Up Craze

By 1989, arcades were in the midst of a cooperative revolution. Beat-'em-ups like Double Dragon had proven that fighting hordes of enemies alongside friends could be exhilarating, and Teenage Mutant Ninja Turtles: The Arcade Game took this concept to a new level by combining popular media with polished, fast-paced gameplay. Developed by Konami, the game allowed up to four players to control the heroes in a half-shell — Leonardo, Michelangelo, Donatello, and Raphael — as they battled the nefarious Foot Clan and their allies across New York City.

The game's narrative was simple yet compelling: the Turtles must rescue their friend April O'Neil and defeat the evil Shredder. This story drove the action forward, providing context for the endless waves of Foot Soldiers, mutant henchmen, and giant bosses players would face. What made the game unique was its blend of accessibility and depth: casual players could pick up a Turtle and start brawling immediately, while dedicated players could master combos, weapon usage, and positioning to maximize damage and survival.

Gameplay revolved around side-scrolling action. Players moved through streets, rooftops, and sewers, striking enemies with punches, kicks, and weapons unique to each Turtle. Health bars and limited continues created tension, encouraging teamwork to survive the increasingly challenging waves of adversaries. Environmental interaction added layers to the gameplay: barrels could be thrown, enemies could be pushed off ledges, and power-ups appeared at strategic intervals to keep the pace frenetic and exciting.

Technologically, the game was impressive for 1989. Detailed, colorful sprites captured the personalities of the Turtles, while smooth animations made combat feel fluid. Enemy AI was aggressive yet readable, allowing players to anticipate attacks while still feeling challenged. The game's music and sound effects, inspired by the TV series, reinforced the cartoonish yet urgent atmosphere, making the arcade experience feel like stepping into a beloved animated world.

Cheat culture and strategy quickly emerged among skilled players. Knowing enemy spawn points, optimal attack sequences, and weapon usage allowed players to conserve health and defeat bosses more efficiently. Coordinating with other players to cover areas, combine attacks, and rescue teammates became essential at higher difficulty levels. The game rewarded both reflexes and cooperative planning, ensuring that each playthrough was engaging and dynamic.

Home ports followed on systems such as the Nintendo Entertainment System, DOS computers, and Sega Genesis. While some compromises were necessary — fewer on-screen enemies, simplified graphics, and reduced multiplayer support — the essence of the arcade experience survived. Players could still punch, kick, and slice through waves of Foot Soldiers, experiencing the thrill of teamwork and chaotic action in their own homes.

Culturally, Teenage Mutant Ninja Turtles: The Arcade Game captured the spirit of the late 80s pop culture boom. It merged the growing popularity of licensed media with innovative cooperative gameplay, creating a game that appealed to both fans of the cartoon and arcade enthusiasts. The title contributed significantly to the beat-'em-up genre, inspiring countless imitators and cementing Konami's reputation as a master of cooperative arcade experiences.

From a design perspective, the game introduced enduring concepts:

Four-player simultaneous cooperative gameplay

Character-specific abilities and weapon mechanics

Environmental interaction to enhance strategic combat

Progressive enemy waves culminating in challenging boss battles

Every jump, strike, and weapon swing mattered. Every player's positioning could determine success or failure. Every boss encounter tested timing, coordination, and tactical thinking.

In 1989, Teenage Mutant Ninja Turtles: The Arcade Game demonstrated the power of combining popular media, cooperative action, and engaging mechanics. It transformed arcades into chaotic, social playgrounds where players could fight together, laugh, and experience the thrill of heroism in a vividly animated New York City.

The Turtles leapt. Foot Soldiers fell. Shredder schemed. And across the arcades, friends learned that together, they could conquer any challenge.

Chapter Twenty-Three - Final Fight and the Rise of the Urban Beat-'Em-Up

By 1989, the beat-'em-up genre had firmly established itself in arcades, but few titles captured the gritty, urban intensity quite like Final Fight, developed by Capcom. Set in the fictional Metro City, Final Fight combined cinematic presentation, tight controls, and relentless enemy waves to immerse players in a violent underworld teeming with gangs, corruption, and chaos.

Players could choose from three heroes: Cody Travers, a street-wise brawler; Guy, a nimble martial artist; and Haggar, a former professional wrestler turned mayor. Each character had distinct strengths: Cody balanced speed and power, Guy excelled in agility and rapid attacks, and Haggar relied on brute strength and grapples. This diversity encouraged both cooperative and competitive play, as players discovered the best strategies to complement one another during the escalating battles through Metro City.

The story, while straightforward — rescue the mayor's daughter Jessica from the Mad Gear gang — served as a backdrop for intense, arcade-style action. Players moved through the streets, subways, and industrial areas, facing waves of enemies that included street thugs, knife-wielding punks, and bizarre bosses with unique attack patterns. Each stage escalated in difficulty, requiring precise timing, situational awareness, and mastery of each character's abilities.

Gameplay revolved around punching, kicking, jumping, and grappling enemies while dodging hazards and projectiles. Weapons scattered throughout stages — knives, pipes, bottles, and swords — added a strategic layer, forcing players to decide when to use them or conserve for critical moments. Environmental hazards, from exploding barrels to deadly drop-offs, further heightened tension and rewarded careful navigation.

Technologically, Final Fight was remarkable. Capcom's arcade hardware allowed for large, detailed sprites, fluid animation, and smooth side-scrolling. Each character's movement felt responsive, and enemies exhibited varied attack patterns that kept players on constant alert. The urban environments were richly designed: graffiti-covered walls, flickering streetlights, and bustling background activity created a sense of living, breathing city streets under siege. Sound effects — grunts, punches, weapon clashes — and a pounding soundtrack reinforced the adrenaline-fueled atmosphere.

Advanced strategies and emergent gameplay quickly became central to Final Fight's culture. Expert players memorized enemy spawn patterns, optimized attack sequences, and coordinated combos in multiplayer sessions. Haggar's grapples could clear groups of enemies efficiently, Guy's speed allowed for hit-and-run tactics, and Cody offered balanced offensive and defensive options. Success often depended on players understanding the strengths of their chosen character while adapting to ever-changing enemy behavior.

Home ports appeared on the Super Nintendo Entertainment System, among others. While these versions had fewer on-screen enemies and slightly simplified graphics, they preserved the intense combat and cooperative mechanics. The SNES port in particular brought Final Fight into living rooms, allowing players to relive the chaos of Metro City with friends and experience one of the era's definitive beat-'em-ups outside of the arcade.

Culturally, Final Fight epitomized the late-80s fascination with gritty, urban action. Its combination of cinematic presentation, intense combat, and multiplayer cooperation influenced countless titles in the beat-'em-up genre. Arcades became arenas where friends tested reflexes, coordinated strategies, and competed for high scores, cementing Final Fight as a cornerstone of arcade gaming culture.

From a design perspective, Final Fight introduced enduring concepts:

Character diversity with unique abilities and playstyles

Environmental hazards integrated into combat for tactical depth

Cooperative multiplayer as a strategic and social experience

Cinematic, immersive urban environments that enhanced narrative tension

Every punch mattered. Every weapon pickup could turn the tide. Every grapple, kick, and jump contributed to survival. Final Fight demanded precision, timing, and teamwork, rewarding players who could adapt quickly to relentless enemies and chaotic stages.

In 1989, Final Fight transformed the beat-'em-up genre, proving that urban violence, cooperative strategy, and cinematic presentation could coexist in a thrilling, addictive arcade experience.

The streets were dangerous. Enemies were relentless. And every hero had to fight their way through Metro City, one punch at a time.

Chapter Twenty-Four – Golden Axe and the Rise of Fantasy Brawlers

By 1989, the beat-'em-up genre had expanded beyond gritty urban streets into imaginative fantasy worlds. Golden Axe, developed by Sega, combined cooperative action with swords, sorcery, and mythical creatures, offering players a rich, visually striking alternative to urban brawlers like Final Fight. Its success showcased how high-octane combat could thrive in settings far removed from city streets.

Players could choose from three heroes: Ax Battler, a swordsman with balanced strength; Tyris Flare, an agile Amazon capable of unleashing powerful fire attacks; and Gilius Thunderhead, a dwarf with devastating axe strikes and brute-force power. Each character's abilities influenced combat strategy: Ax Battler excelled in melee versatility, Tyris used speed and ranged magical attacks, and Gilius could withstand heavy damage while controlling crowds. This diversity encouraged cooperative play and strategic coordination in the fight against waves of enemies and towering bosses.

The story was classic fantasy: a dark lord, Death Adder, has kidnapped the king and threatens the land. Players traverse forests, mountains, castles, and dungeons, battling skeletons, goblins, and monstrous beasts, culminating in epic confrontations with the villain and his elite lieutenants. Each stage presented a mix of hand-to-hand combat, weapon pickups, and magical attacks, offering both immediate action and tactical depth.

Gameplay blended traditional beat-'em-up mechanics with unique fantasy elements. Players could pick up and swing weapons — swords, axes, and clubs — and unleash magic attacks by collecting blue, green, or red potions. Magic attacks varied in power, with some characters able to summon firestorms, lightning strikes, or protective shields. The combination of melee combat, ranged magic, and weapon management added layers of strategy, particularly in cooperative sessions where players coordinated attacks for maximum efficiency.

Technologically, Golden Axe was impressive for Sega's 1989 hardware. Large, colorful sprites depicted heroes, enemies, and detailed environments. Backgrounds were vibrant, featuring waterfalls, castles, and lava pits, while animations emphasized the heft of weapons and the power of magical attacks. Sound effects and a driving soundtrack enhanced immersion, providing cues for enemy actions, spellcasting, and environmental hazards.

Advanced strategies quickly developed within the arcade community. Memorizing enemy spawn patterns, timing attacks for maximum damage, and managing magic resources were key to survival. Players discovered ways to control crowd dynamics, using wide-reaching attacks or coordinated spells to handle multiple enemies simultaneously. Cooperative play demanded communication and strategic planning, making Golden Axe a social as well as an action-oriented experience.

Home ports appeared on the Sega Genesis, Master System, and various computers. While some limitations reduced enemy density or simplified backgrounds, the core gameplay — cooperative melee combat, weapon swings, and magical attacks — remained intact. The home experience allowed players to relive arcade battles in their living rooms, making Golden Axe one of the defining beat-'em-up franchises of the era.

Culturally, Golden Axe captured the imagination of players with its blend of high fantasy and action-packed gameplay. It inspired sequels, spin-offs, and adaptations, reinforcing the viability of cooperative fantasy brawlers. The game's emphasis on teamwork, combined with visually spectacular combat, helped establish a template for fantasy-themed arcade experiences that would endure for decades.

From a design perspective, Golden Axe introduced enduring concepts:

Character-specific abilities, combining melee and magic for strategic depth

Cooperative gameplay that rewarded communication and coordination

Environmental and weapon-based interactions integrated into combat

Fantasy world-building that enhanced immersion and narrative engagement

Every swing of the sword mattered. Every magical spell could turn the tide. Every enemy wave demanded attention, timing, and teamwork. Golden Axe demonstrated that beat-'em-up gameplay could thrive outside urban settings, providing players with a rich, fantastical alternative full of chaos, strategy, and excitement.

In 1989, Golden Axe proved that fantasy and cooperative action could coexist in exhilarating arcade form. The heroes advanced. Enemies fell. Spells flared. And players experienced the joy of teamwork, mythic battles, and unforgettable arcade action.

Chapter Twenty-Five - Double Dragon and the Definitive Side-Scrolling Brawler

By 1987, the arcade scene was dominated by fighting games and platformers, but few titles would redefine cooperative combat as powerfully as Double Dragon, developed by Technōs Japan. Double Dragon took the side-scrolling beat-'em-up formula and perfected it, combining urban storytelling, fluid mechanics, and two-player cooperative gameplay into an experience that became a cornerstone of the genre.

Players assumed the roles of brothers Billy and Jimmy Lee, martial artists on a mission to rescue Billy's kidnapped girlfriend, Marian, from the Black Warriors gang. This narrative — while simple — gave context to relentless street battles across urban landscapes. Players fought their way through alleys, rooftops, and industrial zones, engaging gangs of thugs, knife-wielding enemies, and unique bosses, all while advancing the story in real time.

Gameplay in Double Dragon was groundbreaking for its era. Players could punch, kick, jump, and execute grabs and throws, creating a more dynamic combat experience than most contemporaries. Weapons were scattered throughout stages, including bats, knives, and whips, and could be picked up and used strategically. The two-player cooperative mode allowed friends to coordinate attacks, combine combos, and cover each other's weaknesses, adding depth and excitement rarely seen in other games of the time.

Enemy design was varied and strategic. Regular thugs often attacked in groups, requiring players to manage crowd control, while mini-bosses and stage bosses demanded precise timing, spatial awareness, and clever use of weapons. Patterns emerged for observant players, who could memorize attack sequences to survive the most chaotic encounters. This balance of reactive skill and strategic planning made the game accessible yet challenging.

Technologically, Double Dragon leveraged smooth scrolling, detailed sprite animation, and responsive controls to create fluid, believable combat. Enemy sprites were expressive, depicting pain, aggression, and defeat convincingly. Backgrounds ranged from graffiti-covered alleys to neon-lit streets, establishing a gritty, urban aesthetic that enhanced immersion. Sound effects — punches, kicks, weapon clashes — and the energetic soundtrack punctuated the action, giving each stage an immediate sense of urgency.

Advanced strategies and techniques became a key part of the arcade experience. Skilled players learned to chain throws, time jump kicks, and use weapons efficiently. Cooperative tactics included alternating attacks, setting up opponents for devastating throws, and managing limited resources strategically. These approaches allowed players to maximize efficiency, survive longer, and earn higher scores, turning the game into both a test of reflexes and tactical coordination.

Home ports of Double Dragon appeared on the Nintendo Entertainment System, Sega Master System, and later home computers. While some versions simplified enemy density or reduced frame rates, the core mechanics — cooperative brawling, weapon use, and strategic combat — remained intact. Players could experience the tension and satisfaction of clearing waves of enemies alongside a friend without stepping into an arcade.

Culturally, Double Dragon popularized side-scrolling beat-'em-ups and set a benchmark for cooperative gameplay. Its combination of martial arts action, urban setting, and social interaction influenced countless titles and inspired sequels, adaptations, and homages. The game's simple yet compelling narrative, paired with intense, skill-based action, ensured its lasting impact on both arcades and home gaming.

From a design perspective, Double Dragon introduced enduring concepts:

Cooperative two-player combat with complementary character strategies

Weapon pickups that influenced combat tactics

Enemy patterns that rewarded memorization and strategic planning

Urban environments that enhanced narrative immersion

Every punch counted. Every jump kick had impact. Every coordinated throw between brothers could determine survival. Double Dragon demanded timing, teamwork, and tactical insight, rewarding players who mastered its mechanics with the thrill of dominance over increasingly chaotic street battles.

In 1987, Double Dragon proved that cooperative action, tight mechanics, and engaging urban storytelling could combine to create a definitive arcade experience. The Lee brothers advanced. Enemies fell. Streets were cleared. And players discovered that teamwork, skill, and perseverance were the keys to victory.

Chapter Twenty-Six – Captain Commando and the Futuristic Beat-'Em-Up Revolution

By 1991, beat-'em-ups were evolving beyond gritty streets and fantasy lands into imaginative, futuristic worlds, and Captain Commando, developed by Capcom, became a hallmark of this transformation. Set in Metro City of the near future, the game combined vibrant, colorful graphics, diverse characters, and fast-paced cooperative gameplay, creating an arcade experience that was both chaotic and strategic.

Players could choose from four heroes: Captain Commando, the titular leader with versatile attacks; Mack the Knife, a cyborg with deadly punches and kicks; Ginzu the Ninja, fast and precise; and Baby Head, a child genius in a robotic suit capable of unique aerial attacks. Each character had distinct abilities, strengths, and weaknesses, encouraging cooperative teamwork and strategic play. Unlike prior beat-'em-ups, Captain Commando emphasized character diversity not just for aesthetics but as a core component of gameplay strategy.

The game's story — the evil organization "Mad Gear" has returned to wreak havoc on Metro City — served as a driving force behind relentless combat. Players battled waves of enemies ranging from robotic minions to mutant thugs, culminating in enormous, creatively designed boss encounters. Each stage introduced new hazards, enemy types, and environmental interactions, keeping the gameplay fresh and unpredictable.

Gameplay combined traditional punch-and-kick mechanics with cooperative strategy, weapon pickups, and environmental elements. Players could throw enemies, use melee weapons, or unleash special attacks, including each character's unique "super move" that cleared crowds or inflicted massive damage. The balance between aggressive offense, positioning, and strategic use of abilities was critical, especially in the four-player arcade configuration where chaos escalated quickly.

Technologically, Captain Commando was impressive for its time. Capcom's arcade hardware allowed for large, fluidly animated sprites, detailed backgrounds depicting futuristic cityscapes, and smooth scrolling. Enemy AI was challenging, but predictable enough to reward skill and memorization. Sound design, including character grunts, explosions, and vibrant music tracks, reinforced the action, making each stage feel alive and immersive.

Cheat culture and advanced strategies emerged among dedicated players. Knowledge of enemy spawn points, boss patterns, and optimal use of character abilities allowed skilled teams to progress further and achieve higher scores. Coordinated tactics, such as using Captain Commando to control crowds while Mack or Ginzu targeted ranged threats, highlighted the depth possible in cooperative play. Unlike many beat-'em-ups of the time, Captain Commando rewarded both individual skill and teamwork in equal measure.

Home ports appeared on the Super Nintendo Entertainment System, adapting the arcade's fast-paced, colorful action for living rooms. While the SNES version sometimes reduced on-screen enemies and simplified backgrounds, the cooperative mechanics, character diversity, and dynamic combat were preserved, allowing players to relive the arcade's intensity at home.

Culturally, Captain Commando reinforced the appeal of futuristic beat-'em-ups. Its imaginative setting, memorable characters, and cooperative gameplay made it a standout in arcades worldwide. The game influenced later titles by demonstrating how strong character diversity, cooperative strategy, and visually engaging environments could elevate the genre beyond traditional urban or fantasy settings.

From a design perspective, Captain Commando introduced and refined several enduring concepts:

Diverse characters with unique abilities influencing gameplay strategy

Cooperative mechanics rewarding teamwork and tactical coordination

Environmental hazards and weapon use integrated into combat

Futuristic, cinematic world-building to enhance immersion

Every attack mattered. Every teammate's positioning influenced survival. Every boss encounter demanded timing, strategy, and adaptability. Captain Commando showed that beat-'em-ups could be both chaotic and strategic, offering players the thrill of futuristic combat combined with the satisfaction of coordinated teamwork.

In 1991, Captain Commando proved that imagination, cooperation, and skill could coexist in a futuristic arcade arena. The heroes advanced. Enemies were obliterated. Special attacks flared. And players learned that in a city under siege, teamwork and mastery were the keys to victory.

Chapter Twenty-Seven – Cadillacs and Dinosaurs: Chaos on Wheels

By 1993, arcade beat-'em-ups had reached a point of stylistic and mechanical maturity, blending cooperative action with vibrant settings and inventive enemy designs. Cadillacs and Dinosaurs, developed by Capcom, exemplified this evolution. Based on the comic book series Xenozoic Tales, the game combined environmental storytelling, fast-paced combat, and cooperative gameplay, creating an arcade experience that stood out for its humor, chaos, and creativity.

Players could select from four characters: Jack Tenrec, a versatile and balanced fighter; Hannah Dundee, agile and precise with effective ranged attacks; Mustapha Cairo, a powerful brawler excelling in crowd control; and Mess O'Bradovich, a brutish character capable of devastating grapples. Each character had unique strengths, making team coordination essential, especially as players faced increasingly aggressive waves of enemies and dynamically evolving stages.

The narrative — battling dinosaurs, mutated thugs, and the sinister nefarious gangs who threaten civilization — drove gameplay forward while providing a rich backdrop for imaginative combat. Stages spanned jungles, cities, and industrial zones, often littered with interactive objects like cars, crates, and barrels that could be used both offensively and defensively. Players fought a mix of human and dinosaur foes, each requiring distinct strategies to overcome. Bosses were large, visually striking, and often combined environmental hazards with relentless attacks, challenging players to adapt on the fly.

Gameplay emphasized fast, fluid combat with a focus on both hand-to-hand fighting and tactical use of the environment. Players could punch, kick, throw, and utilize weapons discovered in the stages, while cooperative play encouraged coordinated attacks. Timing, positioning, and efficient crowd management were critical, particularly during intense sequences where multiple enemies attacked simultaneously. The inclusion of dinosaurs as interactive combatants

— sometimes allies, sometimes foes — added unpredictability and excitement to each stage.

Technologically, Cadillacs and Dinosaurs showcased Capcom's late-era arcade hardware. Detailed, colorful sprites, smooth animation, and cinematic camera effects made the action both readable and visually spectacular. Sound design reinforced the chaos: punches, roars, crashes, and explosions combined with an energetic soundtrack to immerse players in a vividly animated world. The game's fast pace and cooperative mechanics kept players engaged while rewarding precision and strategy.

Advanced strategies became essential for high-level play. Players memorized enemy placement, weapon locations, and boss patterns to optimize efficiency. Cooperative strategies included dividing roles — one player clearing crowds while another focused on bosses — and using environmental hazards to maximum effect. Survival depended on adaptability, timing, and understanding each character's strengths in combination with teammates.

Home ports of Cadillacs and Dinosaurs were released on the Super Nintendo Entertainment System and various home computers. While limited by hardware constraints — fewer on-screen enemies, simplified animations, and reduced environmental interaction — the core cooperative gameplay, character diversity, and chaotic fun remained intact. These ports brought the arcade experience to living rooms, allowing players to relive the high-energy action in a home setting.

Culturally, Cadillacs and Dinosaurs reinforced the late-arcade trend of blending licensed properties with innovative gameplay. Its humor, inventive enemy design, and chaotic cooperative mechanics captured players' imaginations, influencing future beat-'em-ups and licensed arcade games. The game demonstrated that creative settings, dynamic environments, and varied characters could elevate cooperative action to new heights.

From a design perspective, Cadillacs and Dinosaurs introduced enduring concepts:

Character diversity emphasizing complementary abilities

Environmental hazards as tactical and interactive tools

Cooperative mechanics rewarding strategy, timing, and coordination

Dynamic, colorful stages that reinforced narrative and gameplay immersion

Every punch, kick, and throw mattered. Every interactive object could change the tide of battle. Every cooperative decision determined survival. Cadillacs and Dinosaurs showcased the potential of imaginative settings and team-based chaos in the beat-'em-up genre.

In 1993, Capcom proved that licensed properties could deliver intense, cooperative arcade action. Dinosaurs rampaged. Foes fell. Players coordinated and strategized. And the arcade world learned that teamwork, creativity, and reflexes could dominate even the wildest of prehistoric battles.

Chapter Twenty-Eight - Streets of Rage: Urban Vigilantes on the Genesis

By 1991, the beat-'em-up genre had fully transitioned to home consoles, and Streets of Rage, developed by Sega for the Genesis, became a landmark in showing that arcade-quality brawls could thrive outside arcades. With slick graphics, a pulsating soundtrack, and deep cooperative gameplay, Streets of Rage brought the gritty urban fight to living rooms worldwide, combining narrative, style, and precise mechanics into an unforgettable experience.

Players chose from three former police officers — Axel Stone, Blaze Fielding, and Adam Hunter — each with unique fighting styles. Axel excelled in balanced attacks and combo potential, Blaze was fast and agile with high jump kicks, and Adam packed brute strength and crowd-control abilities. This diversity encouraged cooperative strategy: two players could complement each other's skills, coordinate attacks, and tackle enemies efficiently while navigating the crime-ridden streets of Metro City.

The story was straightforward yet immersive: a criminal syndicate, led by the mysterious Mr. X, has taken over the city. Players must fight their way through five stages, each populated with gangs, mutant enforcers, and massive bosses, restoring justice to the streets. The urban environments were rich in detail — neon-lit streets, abandoned factories, and dark alleys — creating a world that felt alive, dangerous, and urgent.

Gameplay emphasized fluid combat and strategic movement. Players could punch, kick, jump, grab, and throw enemies while using environmental objects as weapons. Streets of Rage introduced the "special attack" mechanic, allowing players to unleash devastating moves that cleared multiple foes but cost some health, forcing tactical decision-making. Cooperative play allowed for combined attacks and covering teammates, giving a sense of teamwork essential for surviving later levels.

Technologically, Streets of Rage was a showcase for the Genesis hardware. Large, detailed sprites moved smoothly across richly animated backgrounds. Enemy AI was aggressive but predictable, rewarding skillful play and memorization. Yuzo Koshiro's iconic soundtrack combined electronic beats, funk, and techno, providing a dynamic audio backdrop that heightened the sense of tension and action, making each stage feel like a living, breathing urban battleground.

Advanced strategies emerged among expert players. Memorizing enemy spawn patterns, timing combos for crowd control, and managing the use of special attacks became essential for success. Players developed tactics to handle bosses efficiently, often using environmental hazards to gain the upper hand. Cooperative play allowed one player to control groups of enemies while the other targeted more dangerous foes, reinforcing teamwork as a key component of mastery.

The impact of Streets of Rage on home gaming was profound. Unlike many arcade ports, this title was designed with consoles in mind, offering two-player simultaneous gameplay with near-arcade fidelity. It demonstrated that deep, cooperative, skill-based beat-'em-ups could succeed on home systems, paving the way for sequels and influencing countless future titles in the genre.

Culturally, Streets of Rage cemented Sega's reputation as a home-console powerhouse. Its urban aesthetic, memorable characters, and kinetic gameplay captivated players and defined a generation of home beat-'em-ups. The game's music, characters, and style have endured, influencing later brawlers and maintaining a dedicated fanbase even decades after release.

From a design perspective, Streets of Rage introduced enduring concepts:

Character diversity with complementary abilities

Strategic use of special attacks balancing power and health management

Cooperative mechanics rewarding teamwork and coordination

Urban stage design enhancing immersion and narrative tension

Memorable soundtrack reinforcing atmosphere and player engagement

Every punch, every grab, every special attack mattered. Every cooperative strategy could determine survival. Streets of Rage demanded timing, coordination, and mastery of each character's unique abilities, rewarding skillful and thoughtful play.

In 1991, Streets of Rage proved that home consoles could deliver thrilling, cooperative beat-'em-up experiences that rivaled the arcade. The streets were violent. Foes were relentless. Players fought side by side. And the city learned that justice could be reclaimed through teamwork, skill, and sheer determination.

Chapter Twenty-Nine – The Ninja Warriors: Cybernetic Combat Unleashed

By 1987, arcade developers were experimenting with unique gameplay mechanics and larger-than-life characters, and The Ninja Warriors, developed by Taito, became a standout example. Combining side-scrolling beat-'em-up action with towering, cybernetic protagonists, the game delivered an intense cooperative experience that felt futuristic, cinematic, and relentless.

Players controlled one of three super-powered ninja androids — Ninja, Kunoichi, or Kamaitachi — each imbued with distinct abilities. Ninja and Kunoichi were agile and balanced, capable of rapid attacks, while Kamaitachi was slower but delivered devastating blows. This variety encouraged cooperative play, as players had to coordinate movement, timing, and attacks to survive waves of enemy soldiers, robotic foes, and massive bosses that appeared throughout the urban and industrial stages.

The story, while minimal, set the tone: a corrupt government and criminal organization have taken control, and the cybernetic ninja warriors are humanity's last hope. Stages ranged from neon-lit city streets to factories and industrial complexes, often filled with hazards like laser turrets, electrified floors, and moving machinery. The combination of environmental dangers and relentless enemy waves created tension and a sense of urgency rarely seen in contemporaneous beat-'em-ups.

Gameplay emphasized precise timing, positioning, and cooperative strategy. Players could punch, kick, jump, and perform special attacks, combining these abilities with environmental interaction and teamwork. Advanced tactics included staggering enemies to chain attacks, using cooperative throws, and timing jumps to avoid hazards while attacking effectively. The game demanded both reflexes and planning, particularly in later stages where multiple enemy types attacked simultaneously.

Technologically, The Ninja Warriors was impressive for Taito's arcade hardware. Large, imposing sprites conveyed a sense of power and weight, while smooth animation made combat fluid and satisfying. The enemies were diverse in design and behavior, requiring players to adapt continuously. The soundtrack and sound effects reinforced the tension, with pounding beats, robotic noises, and dramatic boss cues immersing players in a futuristic battleground.

Cheat culture and expert strategies emerged quickly. Players memorized enemy spawn points, attack patterns, and environmental hazards to maximize survival. Cooperative strategies were essential: one player could control crowds of weaker enemies while another targeted dangerous foes or bosses, creating dynamic and tactical gameplay that rewarded teamwork and mastery of character abilities.

Home ports eventually appeared on the Super Nintendo Entertainment System and other platforms, though limitations in hardware reduced sprite size and enemy density. Despite this, the core gameplay — towering ninja androids, cooperative combat, and environmental challenges — remained intact, allowing players to experience the arcade's intensity at home.

Culturally, The Ninja Warriors stood out as a unique blend of futuristic design, cooperative strategy, and beat-'em-up mechanics. Its towering protagonists, cinematic style, and cooperative gameplay influenced later action games and helped solidify Taito's reputation as an innovative arcade developer. The game demonstrated that beat-'em-ups could explore imaginative settings, larger-than-life characters, and tactical depth while maintaining thrilling, fast-paced action.

From a design perspective, The Ninja Warriors introduced enduring concepts:

Distinct character abilities influencing cooperative strategy

Environmental hazards integrated into combat for added challenge

Towering, cinematic character design enhancing player immersion

Cooperative gameplay emphasizing teamwork, timing, and coordination

Every punch mattered. Every jump, every throw, every cooperative maneuver could determine survival. The Ninja Warriors demanded reflexes, coordination, and strategic thinking, rewarding players who mastered both individual skill and team dynamics.

In 1987, The Ninja Warriors proved that side-scrolling beat-'em-ups could be futuristic, cinematic, and cooperative while maintaining intense, relentless action. The androids advanced. Enemies fell. Hazards loomed. And players discovered that precision, timing, and teamwork were the keys to victory in a cybernetic world.

Chapter Thirty - Warriors of Fate: Legendary Battles in the Arcades

By 1992, the beat-'em-up genre had reached its peak in arcades, blending cooperative gameplay, cinematic presentation, and immersive historical settings. Warriors of Fate, developed by Capcom, epitomized this evolution. Inspired by the classic Chinese tale Romance of the Three Kingdoms, the game combined fast-paced side-scrolling combat with strategic depth, historical flair, and cooperative multiplayer excitement, providing a grand finale for the era of arcade brawlers.

Players could choose from multiple heroes, each with unique fighting styles, strengths, and abilities. The primary characters — Kenshiro, Lu Bu, and Zhao Yun — offered diverse combat approaches: balanced attacks, rapid strikes, or overwhelming power moves. This variety encouraged cooperation, as players coordinated to manage waves of enemies, exploit boss weaknesses, and navigate the increasingly complex stages that spanned war-torn villages, fortresses, and battlefields.

The story was epic in scope: players assumed the roles of heroic generals battling against the tyrannical forces threatening the Han Dynasty. Each stage presented unique challenges, from hordes of enemy soldiers to massive bosses inspired by legendary figures of Chinese history. Environmental hazards, siege equipment, and interactive objects added layers of tactical decision-making to the frenetic combat, requiring both individual skill and teamwork to succeed.

Gameplay emphasized fluid combat, crowd management, and cooperative coordination. Players could punch, kick, grab, throw, and unleash powerful special moves. Weapon pickups, from spears to swords, allowed for dynamic combat strategies, while cooperative tactics — timing combined attacks, staggering enemies, and controlling space — were essential to survive the larger-scale battles of later stages. The game rewarded mastery of each character's abilities and knowledge of enemy behavior, creating depth uncommon for the time.

Technologically, Warriors of Fate was a marvel of Capcom's arcade hardware. Large, detailed sprites and richly animated backgrounds brought historical battlefields to life, while smooth animation and responsive controls made combat feel dynamic and satisfying. Enemy AI was challenging but predictable enough for players to develop advanced strategies. The music and sound effects, inspired by epic orchestral and traditional motifs, enhanced the historical immersion and gave each stage a cinematic intensity.

Advanced strategies emerged quickly among experienced players. Knowledge of enemy placement, boss attack patterns, and optimal use of weapons and special attacks was critical. Cooperative play allowed one player to focus on controlling crowds while another targeted dangerous foes or bosses, emphasizing teamwork as a core element of success. Timing, positioning, and communication between players could mean the difference between victory and defeat.

Home ports appeared on the Super Nintendo Entertainment System and other systems. While hardware limitations reduced sprite size and stage complexity, the essence of Warriors of Fate — cooperative combat, character diversity, and historical immersion — remained intact. Players could experience the thrill of leading legendary warriors into battle without stepping into an arcade.

Culturally, Warriors of Fate reinforced the appeal of cooperative beat-'em-ups with narrative depth and historical context. Its combination of strategy, action, and cinematic presentation left a lasting impression on players and influenced future arcade and console brawlers. The game demonstrated that beat-'em-ups could be both intellectually engaging and viscerally exciting, blending skill, teamwork, and story into a single package.

From a design perspective, Warriors of Fate introduced enduring concepts:

Diverse heroes with unique abilities influencing cooperative strategy

Integration of weapons and environmental hazards for tactical depth

Epic, historically inspired stages that enhanced immersion

Cooperative gameplay emphasizing timing, positioning, and teamwork

Cinematic presentation and musical scoring to elevate the arcade experience

Every strike mattered. Every coordinated attack could turn the tide. Every boss encounter demanded skill, timing, and cooperation. Warriors of Fate rewarded players who mastered both the mechanics and the art of teamwork, providing a satisfying conclusion to the beat-'em-up experience of the era.

In 1992, Warriors of Fate proved that cooperative side-scrolling brawlers could combine historical storytelling, cinematic presentation, and intense combat into a thrilling arcade experience. Heroes advanced. Armies fell. Bosses were defeated. And players discovered that skill, strategy, and teamwork were the ultimate keys to victory on the battlefield.

www.ingramcontent.com/pod-product-compliance
Lightning Source LLC
LaVergne TN
LVHW100307210926
848480LV00003B/1052
9798215622070